THE COMPLETE VISUAL ENCYCLOPEDIA OF

NAVAL AIRCRAFT
OF WORLD WARS I AND II

THE COMPLETE VISUAL ENCYCLOPEDIA OF
NAVAL AIRCRAFT
OF WORLD WARS I AND II

Features a directory of over 70 aircraft with 330 identification photographs

Shipborne fighters, bombers and flying boats, including the Curtiss Helldiver,
Mitsubishi Zero-Sen, Supermarine Seafire, and many more

Francis Crosby

LORENZ BOOKS

This edition is published by Lorenz Books

an imprint of Anness Publishing Ltd

108 Great Russell Street

London WC1B 3NA

info@anness.com

www.lorenzbooks.com

www.annesspublishing.com

Anness Publishing has a new picture agency outlet for images for publishing, promotions
or advertising. Please visit our website www.practicalpictures.com for more information.

A CIP catalogue record for this book is available from the British Library.

Publisher: Joanna Lorenz
Senior Editor: Felicity Forster
Copy Editor: Will Fowler
Cover Design: Ian Sandom
Designer: Design Principals
Production Controller: Ben Worley

Previously published as part of a larger volume,
The World Encyclopedia of Naval Aircraft

PUBLISHER'S NOTE

Although the information in this book is believed to be accurate and true at the time
of going to press, neither the authors nor the publisher can accept any legal responsibility
or liability for any errors or omissions that may have been made.

PAGE 1: **Heinkel He 115B.**
PAGE 2: **Curtiss SOC Seagull.**
PAGE 3: **Vought F4U Corsair.**
OPPOSITE: **Blohm und Voss Bv 138.**

Contents

Introduction

In 1910, Eugene Ely became the first pilot to launch from a ship when he took off from the USS *Birmingham* and landed nearby after just five minutes in the air. On January 18, 1911, Ely became the first to land on a stationary ship – the USS *Pennsylvania* anchored on the waterfront in San Francisco. From these experimental beginnings was born one of the most potent manifestations of military might – naval air power.

Naval aviation during World War I principally took the form of flying boats such as the Curtiss H Series aircraft, and floatplanes operating from modified ships that would crane them to and from the sea's surface. Towards the end of World War I some daring raids saw landplanes taking off from experimental British carriers, but the first US Navy aircraft carrier did not appear until 1922, while three years later Japan launched the very first purpose-designed aircraft carrier.

The design and development of naval combat aircraft has always been challenging. In the early days of military aviation, naval aircraft were built by simply modifying existing land-based aircraft and making them suitable for the harsh environment of carrier operations. Unfortunately, the addition of essential equipment such as arrester hooks and beefed-up undercarriages, as well as strengthened structures, frequently eroded the performance an aircraft may have enjoyed as a landplane. This led to a built-in inferiority compared to land-based types.

TOP: **The Grumman Hellcat, a fine example of a plane designed from the outset as a naval aircraft created to operate from aircraft carriers.**

ABOVE: **Early experiments on ships converted to aircraft carriers led to a new war-winning form of military might – naval air power.**

Purpose-designed naval aircraft such as torpedo-bombers, though potent in their own role, were vulnerable once within range of higher-performance fighters. Only when naval aviation proved its strategic value in World War II did purpose-designed high-performance combat aircraft start to appear that could hold their own over water or land. As a result, naval aviation became a war-winning factor, although unit cost also added to the difficulties faced by naval aircraft designers due to the size of naval aircraft production runs compared to those of land-based aircraft.

LEFT: **The Fairey Swordfish is one of the all-time classic naval combat aircraft. One of the type's many claims to fame is that it was one of the few fighting aircraft in service at both the outbreak and the end of World War II.**
BELOW: **Flying boats like the Consolidated Coronado could patrol vast areas of ocean in search of enemy shipping and submarines. The heyday of the military flying boat was World War II, but many types continued in post-war service.**

BELOW: **Like the Swordfish, the Nakajima B5N was a torpedo-bomber, and as such had the capability to sink even the largest enemy ships and turn the course of a battle. The B5N played a major part in the Japanese attack on Pearl Harbor in December 1941, and went on to sink a number of US aircraft carriers in the Pacific theatre.**

Despite the cost, during World War II aircraft carriers and naval air power enabled nations such as the US, Japan and Britain to project their military power anywhere they could safely sail their carriers. These vast ships, some as complex as small cities, enabled World War II military planners to field potent strike forces many miles from home, and launch attacks around the world.

This book tells the story of naval aviation from the pioneering and proving days of World War I through to the end of World War II, when it became a strategic requirement. The information and data included in the book relate to a range of naval combat aircraft types, such as fighters and torpedo bombers. The reader will also find information about seaplanes, floatplanes and flying boats.

The author had to make difficult choices, and the A–Z listing does not claim to feature every naval aircraft from the period. It does, however, present the individual stories of the aircraft that the author believes to have been the most significant. Specifications are presented in a standard form to enable the reader to make comparisons of weight, speed, armament etc. Some early aircraft are given an endurance rather than a range, and for other older types, details could simply not be found. The performance figures quoted are to give a broad indication of an aircraft's capabilities, which can vary considerably even within the same marks of a type. The carriage of torpedoes and drop tanks can affect performance; even radio aerials can reduce top speed. Thus, the values should be seen as representative, not definitive.

A History of Naval Aircraft in World Wars I and II

Combat aircraft have played an increasingly important role in conflict since they came into their own during the pioneering days of air warfare in World War I. Naval aviation, that is military aviation that takes place from fighting ships, was born in 1911 when a Curtiss biplane landed on a wooden platform built on the cruiser USS *Pennsylvania* and took off from it again. Although seen by most more as a stunt than a demonstration of the potential of naval air power, it proved the concept. The first true carrier with an unobstructed flight deck did not enter service with the Royal Navy until the last stages of World War I, but by the end of World War II the carrier was seen to be a mighty warship with the potential to project a nation's power more flexibly than the large battleships that once ruled the waves.

The power of aircraft carriers and the ability to patrol and dominate vast tracts of ocean with long-range flying boats were both proven in World War II. It was aircraft carriers that enabled the Japanese attack on Pearl Harbor, and carrier-borne aircraft played a major role in the pivotal Battle of Midway, in which four Japanese aircraft carriers were destroyed.

LEFT: **The photograph, taken on the deck of a World War II British carrier, shows over 20 Corsair fighters with wings folded to save space and carrying auxiliary fuel drop tanks. The Royal Navy was the first service to operate the bent-wing fighter from carriers.**

Fleet fighters – the rise of naval air power

Naval air power has its origins in 1910, a key year in the development of military aviation. On November 14 that year, a Curtiss biplane became the first ever to take off from a ship. The aircraft, flown by Eugene B. Ely, flew from a 25.3m/83ft platform built over the bows of the US Navy cruiser USS *Birmingham*. Within two months, Ely had succeeded in landing a Curtiss on a ship, this time the USS *Pennsylvania*. Although these feats were seen by many as little more than stunts, Ely had shown that aircraft actually did not need to operate from dry land. By combining one of the oldest means of transport, the boat, with the newest, the aeroplane, a new means of waging war was born.

Britain's first deck take-off came on January 10, 1912, when the Royal Navy officer Lt C.R. Samson flew a Short biplane from staging erected over the gun turret of the cruiser HMS *Africa*. By 1915, Britain had two ships with 36.6m/120ft-long flying-off decks but they were far from operational. Flying-off platforms were, however, fitted to a handful of Royal Navy ships. A Sopwith Pup, using the HMS *Yarmouth* flying platform, was launched against and destroyed a German Zeppelin – this action is believed to have been the earliest use of a 'carrier-borne' fighter for air defence.

The first significant use of carrier-borne air power came in the 1931–32 war between China and Japan. In January 1932, carrier-borne aircraft operated in support of Japanese land forces in action near Shanghai. It was not, however, until World War II that aircraft carriers and their fighters came into their own.

The carrier was vital in the Japanese campaigns in World War II in the Pacific and enabled them to project power over vast distances. Carriers were able to make or break campaigns

TOP: **The Royal Navy was keen to field the best available fighters to counter the Zeppelin threat at sea. The foredeck of HMS *Furious* is seen here in 1918 with Sopwith Camels brought up from the below-deck hangar by the forward elevator, the opening for which can be seen in the foreground.**
ABOVE: **Aircraft were used for a variety of tasks at sea and on land from the earliest days of air power. Just as aircraft were used to 'spot' artillery on land, here an Italian flying boat helps an Italian Navy vessel direct its fire, circa 1918.**

by providing strike aircraft, and air cover for other ships, convoys and assault ships, and so their protection was vital. Each carrier had fighter aircraft to defend the ships and carriers from air attack. The US Navy developed defensive fighter 'nets' over carrier groups to protect them from enemy aircraft by a combination of radar early-warning and standing patrols of fighters, some up to 64km/40 miles away from the carrier. The carrier that could be protected from air attack was a massive strategic asset in any theatre of war.

While Britain at first had second-rate or obsolete aircraft deployed as carrier-borne fighters, other nations developed high-performance hard-hitting fighters designed from the outset as carrier aircraft. One of the first true fighters deployed by the Royal Navy was the Sea Hurricane, the navalized version of the famous Battle of Britain fighter. RAF Hurricanes had flown on and off HMS *Glorious* during the Norwegian campaign in 1940 and shown that high-performance fighters could be operated from carriers. It was followed into Royal Navy service by the American-built Grumman Martlet (known as the Wildcat in the US Navy and later in the Royal Navy). The Wildcat proved itself almost immediately in its first carrier deployment on convoy protection in September 1941 by driving away or destroying enemy aircraft. Meanwhile, the Sea Hurricanes soldiered on tackling German torpedo aircraft while newer high-performance fighters were awaited from America.

World War II Japanese carrier-borne air power was formidable. Six aircraft carriers took part in the devastating December 1941 attack on Pearl Harbor which decimated the US Pacific Fleet. In this and other attacks, Japanese strike aircraft were only able to carry out their deadly missions because they were escorted by fighters like the Mitsubishi Zero, which took on defending fighters. The Zero was a formidable fighter but its excellent manoeuvrability was achieved at the price of pilot safety. To save weight there was no armour protecting the pilot and often there was not even a radio fitted in the aircraft.

One carrier fighter in particular could be described as a war winner – the Grumman F6F Hellcat. Following its arrival in combat in August 1943, this tough fighter was able to turn the tables on the Zero and gave US Navy and Marine Corps pilots the upper hand until the war's end. Aircraft carriers were shown to be as good as their defences, and in particular the fighters that protected them.

TOP: **Naval air power was at first manifested by aircraft launched like this Sopwith Camel from a launching platform on the Royal Australian Navy ship HMAS *Sydney*, 1917.** ABOVE: **Another favoured method of getting the early naval fighter airborne was by launching them from high-speed lighters. The theory was that if the lighter and its aircraft were already travelling at speed, the wind would lift the aircraft into the air much quicker. The same principle applied to the lighters that were towed at around 25 knots behind a warship – this configuration is pictured with a Sopwith Camel getting airborne.**
BELOW: **The Grumman Hellcat was the second-largest single-engine fighter of World War II after the land-based P-47. The Hellcat was so big because the US Navy needed a fast aircraft that could carry useful loads of weaponry over great distances – this required a large engine and room for lots of fuel.**

Naval aircraft technology up to 1945

When the Wright brothers built their pioneering Wright Flyer in 1903, the principal material used for the wings and fuselage was wood braced by piano wire for added strength. By the end of World War II, just over four decades later, most military aircraft were all-metal and could cover distances and achieve speeds of which the Wrights could have only dreamed.

As engine technology improved and aircraft speeds increased, drag on early aircraft became a serious design consideration and aircraft frames were increasingly covered and enclosed with taut fabric to achieve streamlining. This technique was used into the mid-1930s, but by the time of World War II most new aircraft were of all-metal 'monocoque' construction. Whereas the early fabric-covered aircraft got their structural strength from taut metal bracing wires, the metal skin of the monocoque fuselage, and in time the wings and tail, welded or riveted to a light metal interior framework provided an incredibly strong construction. The downside of this construction was the damage that would be caused by cannon shells hitting the metal structure – in fabric-covered aircraft the shells could have passed right through the aircraft causing little damage.

The Wrights chose a biplane configuration for their Flyer and this form was used in all early naval aircraft, as two pairs of wings generated much more lift than a monoplane. It was not until 1936, for example, that the Royal Air Force deployed a monoplane in front-line service and some time later that the Royal Navy's Fleet Air Arm followed suit.

Until World War II, most carrier-borne fighter aircraft were just navalized versions of proven landplanes. Undercarriages had to be strengthened due to the great stresses generated as an aircraft slammed down on a pitching carrier deck – more early Seafires were written off by landing incidents than by enemy action. The addition of arrester hooks also required strengthening of the fuselage to cope with the violence of 'catching the wire'. As military planners came to realize the war-winning strategic value of aircraft carriers, dedicated purpose-designed naval types began to enter service.

In terms of space saving, wings needed to fold to minimize the room taken up by an aircraft on or below a carrier deck. Wing-folding was a labour-intensive manual task until complex

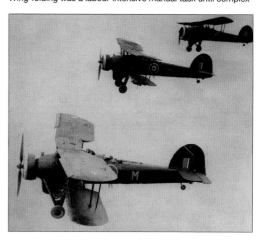

ABOVE: **The Fairey Swordfish is a naval aviation legend. The comparatively slow biplane carried out countless daring missions during World War II against the toughest odds and went on to outlast the aircraft developed to succeed it.**
LEFT: **The superstructure of HMS *Furious* shows just how skilled the pilots of the pictured Sopwith Pups had to be during these early deck operations. Equally primitive at this time was the use of cranes to lift the aircraft from and return them to the hangar below the deck. The development of hydraulic lifts changed this.**

LEFT: **Not all naval aircraft needed a flight deck. Many fighting ships carried small flying boats or amphibians like the Supermarine Walrus or floatplanes such as the Vought Kingfisher pictured. The aircraft would be craned over the side into the sea and then craned back on deck after its mission.**

ABOVE: **The arrester hook was a comparatively simple but effective means of stopping an aircraft in a controlled manner on a carrier deck. Failure to 'catch' any of the wires on landing would result in a punishing meeting with an emergency catcher 'net' that was deployed on later wartime carriers. The other possibilities were a disastrous collision with other aircraft on the deck or going over the side.**
LEFT: **The Grumman Wildcat. Initially known by the Royal Navy as the Martlet, this aircraft was the standard US naval fighter from 1942–43. In December 1940, the aircraft became the first US type in British service in World War II to down an enemy aircraft.**
BELOW: **The Supermarine Walrus served with both the Royal Navy and the Royal Air Force. RN aircraft were amphibian shipborne observation aircraft while the RAF machines were used mainly for Air Sea Rescue missions and saved many lives.**

hydraulic wing-folding systems were developed. Wings could fold a little, i.e. just the wingtips (such as on early Seafires), while others (such as on the Corsair) folded perhaps halfway along their length just outboard of the undercarriage. The Grumman Wildcat's innovative 'sto-wing' mechanism developed by Leroy 'Roy' Grumman was crucial to the US Navy's success in the Pacific in World War II. With the wings folded parallel to the aircraft fuselage in one sweeping motion, the aircraft's size was dramatically reduced. This allowed easier movement around the ship but most significantly increased the carrier's aircraft capacity by 50 per cent. One technical innovation dramatically increased US naval air power. This innovation was used on later Grumman aircraft including the Avenger and Hellcat.

Engine technology developed rapidly between the wars. The 1917 Sopwith Camel had a top speed of 188kph/117mph and was powered by a Clerget 130hp in-line piston engine. Just over a quarter of a century later, the Pratt & Whitney Double Wasp was producing 2,100hp and pushing the Grumman Bearcat along at 677kph/421mph.

At the end of World War I, air-cooled radials and in-line piston-engines were the dominant engine types and both had

much to commend them. They were developed to the maximum until the jet engine ultimately replaced them both, but naval jets were not introduced until after World War II.

Naval aircraft weaponry to 1945

In the early days of air warfare, aircraft armament was non-existent or locally improvised. The first fighters were armed with revolvers, rifles or shotguns carried by the pilots or observers but the importance of reliable hard-hitting armament was soon appreciated. Once weapons like the 0.303in Lewis machine-gun were proven, their use was then perfected. At first the guns were mounted on pivot pins or flexible mounts, aimed by the observers or pilots at enemy aircraft, but they became truly effective once the guns were fixed to the aircraft and were synchronized to fire between the spinning propeller blades. To aim at a target, the pilot simply had to fly straight at it.

During World War I, two rifle-calibre machine-guns were usually enough to inflict serious damage on fabric-covered, mainly wooden aircraft or enemy airships. By the mid-1930s this was clearly inadequate to destroy the larger metal aircraft coming off drawing boards at the time. Consequently, more and bigger guns were used to arm fighter aircraft, and wing-mounted guns and, later, cannon became more common.

During World War I, experiments had been carried out to see if large calibre weapons (cannon) firing explosive ammunition could destroy enemy aircraft. Early British tests found that the recoil of these comparatively large weapons was enough to stop a slow-moving firing aircraft in flight, never mind inflict damage on an enemy. French development work was more successful and a 37mm cannon was used in combat by French aces Guynemer and Fonck, both of whom destroyed German aircraft with the weapon.

TOP: **A Fleet Air Arm Fairey Albacore being armed with 113kg/250lb bombs. Although carrier-based aircraft were frequently used to attack land targets, strikes on shipping with free-fall bombs required great skill and nerve as the attackers were typically met with robust anti-aircraft defences.** ABOVE: **Many naval fighter aircraft, including this Grumman Hellcat, were armed only with machine-guns, in this case six 0.5in Brownings. The picture shows the barrels of the guns being 'pulled through' to ensure they are clear of any obstructions that might cause a jam in combat when failures could prove fatal.**

When the legendary Spitfire first went to war its original armament was eight 0.303in Browning machine-guns but as the Luftwaffe provided their aircraft with more armour and self-sealing fuel tanks it was apparent that eight machine-guns were not adequate to inflict enough damage on enemy aircraft. When the Seafire was developed for production it was

LEFT: **The Fairey Swordfish was typically armed with an 18in torpedo as shown but could also carry the equivalent weight in bombs or mines.**

cannon-armed. Although the machine-gun and cannon were the most significant air-to-air weapons in the period, unguided rockets were highly developed by the end of World War II.

Bombs of varying types and weights were carried from the earliest days of naval aviation. Britain's early bombing successes began on October 8, 1914, with the Royal Naval Air Service raids on the Zeppelin sheds at Dusseldorf and Cologne. The aircraft used were two Sopwith Tabloids. The aircraft attacking Cologne failed to find its target due to bad weather and bombed the railway station instead but the other Tabloid successfully dropped a small number of 9kg/20lb bombs on the airship shed destroying it and Zeppelin Z.9 in the process.

Dedicated carrier-borne torpedo-bombers existed almost exclusively prior to and during World War II in which they played a key role in many actions including the attack at Taranto and the Japanese attack on Pearl Harbor. Torpedo-carrying aircraft had first appeared during the later years of World War I. Generally, the torpedoes carried by these aircraft for attacks on shipping were designed specially for air launch and were smaller and lighter than those carried by submarines. Nevertheless, airborne torpedoes could weigh as much as 908kg/2,000lb, which was more than twice the typical bomb load of a contemporary single-engined bomber. The aircraft carrying it had to be bigger and needed to have a more powerful engine but none were high-performance aircraft and they were vulnerable to fighters. The introduction of improved torpedoes and anti-shipping missiles that could be carried by conventional long-range bombers led to the torpedo-bomber's general disappearance almost immediately after the war.

INSET ABOVE: **A Grumman Corsair shown firing rocket projectiles (RPs) at a Japanese ground target on Okinawa.** BELOW: **A Fleet Air Arm Fairey Firefly armed with cannon and RPs. The high-speed unguided rockets proved deadly on impact with aircraft but were equally devastating against ground targets, armour and surface vessels. Two British RP types were used in World War II – the 6in with 27kg/60lb warhead and the 3.44in with 11kg/25lb warhead.**

Pearl Harbor

The December 7, 1941, Japanese carrier-borne attack on the US naval base at Pearl Harbor was the culmination of ten years of deteriorating relations between the two nations. In 1937 Japan had attacked China as part of its plans to dominate the Far East and South-east Asia. When war broke out in Europe, Japan allied itself with Germany. Meanwhile, the US applied diplomatic pressure and used embargoes to try to resolve Japan's conflict with China. The US oil embargo was particularly badly received in Tokyo where the act was viewed as a threat to Japan's national security. The posturing and pronouncements by both Japan and the US escalated to dangerous levels by the summer of 1941 when the pride and prestige of both nations was in jeopardy. While they both apparently continued to pursue diplomatic means to resolve their differences, Japan already had plans for war.

The Japanese attack on Pearl Harbor was intended to immobilize the US Pacific Fleet so the US could not interfere with Japan's expansionist plans. The attack was conceived by Admiral Isoroku Yamamoto, Commander-in-Chief of the Japanese Combined Fleet, who knew that Japan's only hope of success against the United States and its industrial might was to achieve a swift and overwhelming victory thereby avoiding a prolonged war with a formidable foe.

> "Yesterday, December 7, 1941 – a date which will live in infamy – the United States of America was suddenly and deliberately attacked by naval and air forces of the Empire of Japan."
> **President Franklin Roosevelt**

TOP: **Part of the armada of Japanese aircraft destined for Pearl Harbor prepare to take off from the deck of a Japanese carrier. Total surprise was achieved in the attack that came to be known as 'The Day of Infamy'. Using aircraft operating from more than 322km/200 miles away from the target, the attack required considerable co-ordination.** ABOVE: **Japanese planning for the attack was meticulous and took many forms. Reconnaissance and intelligence received from spies enabled the Japanese military planners to build accurate models with which to brief aircrew. However, this incredibly accurate scale model of Battleship Row was constructed after the attack for use in the making of a Japanese propaganda film.**

On November 26, 1941, a Japanese fleet of 33 warships, including six aircraft carriers, sailed from Japan towards the Hawaiian Islands taking a route to the north to keep it clear of shipping that could alert the US of the Japanese activity. In the early morning of December 7 the fleet found itself about 370km/230 miles north of its target and at 06:00 the first wave of fighters, bombers and torpedo-bombers was launched. Their target at Pearl Harbor was the 130 ships of the US Pacific Fleet. Seven of the Fleet's nine battleships were conveniently berthed together on 'Battleship Row' on the south-east shore of Ford Island. At 06:40 a Japanese midget submarine was spotted and destroyed near the entrance to Pearl Harbor.

ABOVE: **A Japanese Navy Nakajima B5N2 'Kate' takes off from the aircraft carrier *Shokaku*. Nearing the target, the Japanese force split so some of the aircraft could neutralize any attempted defence from US fighter aircraft. Few defending aircraft had the opportunity to leave the ground during the attack.**
ABOVE RIGHT: **Japanese Navy Aichi 'Val' dive-bombers prepare to take off on the morning of December 7, 1941. The carrier in the background is the *Soryu*. A mixed force of 183 bombers, dive-bombers, torpedo-bombers and fighters comprised the first Japanese attack wave that began its take-off at 06:00 hours.**

A few minutes later a US radar station picked up a signal indicating a large formation of aircraft heading their way but interpreted it as a flight of B-17 bombers arriving from the mainland. Within an hour all became clear as the first wave of Japanese aircraft arrived and attacked. In all, 351 Japanese aircraft took part in the attack, including Aichi D3A dive-bombers, Nakajima B5Ns (carrying bombs and torpedoes) and Mitsubishi Zeros.

A large armour-piercing bomb penetrated the deck of the USS *Arizona* which caused one of the ship's ammunition magazines to explode at 08:10. Within nine minutes the *Arizona* sank, with the loss of 1,177 crew. The USS *Oklahoma*, subjected to continued torpedo attack, rolled over, trapping over 400 of her crew inside the hull. Meanwhile, the USS *California* and USS *West Virginia* both sank where they were moored. The USS *Utah*, a training ship, capsized with over 50 of her crew. The USS *Maryland*, USS *Pennsylvania* and USS *Tennessee* all suffered major damage. As well as attacking the harbour itself, Hickam, Wheeler and Bellows airfields, Ewa Marine Corps Air Station and Kaneohe Bay Naval Air Station were all attacked. By the end of the day, 164 US aircraft were destroyed with a further 159 damaged.

The second wave of the Japanese attack came at 08:40, this time destroying the USS *Shaw*, USS *Sotoyomo* and heavily damaging the *Nevada*. By 10:00 the second wave of attacking aircraft had departed having lost only 29 aircraft in the whole raid.

The attack was audacious and, as expected, achieved complete surprise. It also would not have been possible without carrier-borne attack aircraft. It inflicted massive material damage on the Pacific Fleet although the US aircraft carriers were not in port at the time of the attack. The major effect, however, was not what the Japanese had expected.

ABOVE: **The attack on the US Pacific Fleet was intended to warn the US off but instead made the industrial giant more determined to quash Japan.**
BELOW: **Crippled and effectively destroyed by an armour-piercing bomb dropped from a Japanese aircraft, the USS *Arizona* was lost with 1,177 crew. Today, a 56m/184ft-long memorial to those who died during the attack is positioned over the mid-portion of the sunken battleship.**

Tokyo had hoped that the US would take the message and not interfere with Japanese plans in the Western Pacific. Instead the attack on Pearl Harbor united a nation previously divided over the issue of military intervention. The US, incensed at the apparently mock negotiations going on while the attack was imminent, was at war with Japan. When he heard about the botched diplomatic activity that was still going on while the attack was underway, Admiral Yamamoto is supposed to have said, "I fear all we have done is to awaken a sleeping giant and fill him with a terrible resolve."

The Doolittle Raid

The April 1942 US air attack on Japan, launched from the aircraft carrier USS *Hornet* and led by Lieutenant Colonel James H. Doolittle, was at that point the most daring operation undertaken by the United States in the Pacific War. Though conceived as a diversion that would also boost American and Allied morale, the raid generated strategic benefits that far outweighed its limited goals.

The raid had its origins in a chance remark that it might be possible to launch twin-engined bombers from the deck of an aircraft carrier, making feasible an early retaliatory air attack on Japan that would not call for putting even more US warships at risk, close to Japan. On hearing of the idea in January 1942, US Fleet commander Admiral Ernest J. King and Air Forces leader General Henry H. 'Hap' Arnold, responded enthusiastically. Arnold assigned Doolittle to assemble and lead the air group. The well-tested and proven B-25 Mitchell medium bomber was selected and tests showed that it could indeed fly off a carrier while carrying bombs and enough fuel to reach and attack Japan, and then continue on to friendly China.

Recruiting volunteer aircrews for the top-secret mission, Doolittle began special training for his men and modifications to their aircraft. The new carrier *Hornet* was sent to the Pacific to carry out the Navy's part of the mission, which was so secret, her commanding officer, Captain Mitscher, had no idea of his ship's part in the operation until just before 16 B-25s

ABOVE: **Lt Col James H. Doolittle (centre) flanked by members of the crews who took part in the raid and Chinese officials pictured in China after the mission.**

LEFT: **Following the raid, Doolittle expected that the loss of all 16 aircraft, coupled with the relatively minor damage caused to the enemy would lead to his court martial. Instead Doolittle was awarded the Medal of Honor by President Roosevelt and was promoted straight to Brigadier General, missing the rank of Colonel. He went on to command the Twelfth Air Force in North Africa, the Fifteenth Air Force in the Mediterranean and the Eighth Air Force in the UK during the following three years.**

were loaded on his flight deck. *Hornet* sailed on April 2, 1942, and headed west to be joined in mid-ocean on April 13 by USS *Enterprise*, which would provide limited air cover.

The plan called for an afternoon launch on April 18, around 643km/400 miles from Japan but enemy vessels were spotted before dawn on April 18. The small enemy boats were believed to have radioed Japan with details of the American carriers heading their way, so Doolittle's Raiders were forced to take off immediately while still more than 965km/600 miles from their target.

ABOVE LEFT: A B-25 leaves the flight deck of *Hornet*, heading for Japan. Note the personnel watching from the signal lamp platform on the right. For the duration of the voyage leading to the raid, the aircraft were ranged on *Hornet*'s flight deck in the order they were to leave as there was no room to rearrange them. The B-25's long non-folding wings meant they were too large to fit on the elevator to take them below. The lead aircraft, flown by Doolittle himself, had only a few hundred feet of deck to reach take-off speed. ABOVE RIGHT: Smoke pours from Japanese targets following the raid. LEFT: The B-25s were stripped of some of their defensive guns and given extra fuel tanks to extend their range. Wooden broom handles were placed in each plane's plastic tail cone, simulating extra machine-guns to deter enemy fighters. Each B-25 carried four 227kg/500lb bombs. One bomb was decorated with Japanese medals, donated by a US Navy Lieutenant who had received them during pre-war naval attaché service and now wished to return them. BELOW: The B-25 Mitchell went on to become one of the most widely used aircraft of World War II and served with many nations.

Most of the 16 B-25s, each with a crew of five, attacked the Tokyo area, while some bombed Nagoya. Damage to Japanese military targets was slight, and none of the aircraft reached China although virtually all the crews survived.

Japan's military leaders were nevertheless horrified and embarrassed by the audacious raid. The Americans had attacked the home islands once and could do it again and so the Japanese were forced to keep more ships and aircraft near the home islands ready to repulse further US attacks. These significant military resources could otherwise have been used against American forces as they attacked island after island while making their way closer to Japan.

Combined Fleet commander Admiral Isoroku Yamamoto proposed that the Japanese remove the risk of any similar American raids by destroying America's aircraft carriers in the Pacific theatre. The Doolittle raid thus precipitated the Japanese disaster at the Battle of Midway a month and a half later.

Perhaps the most significant result of the logistically impressive Doolittle mission was the hard-to-quantify but very real effect that it had on the morale of the broader American public. The United States was finally hitting back after Pearl Harbor and the brave men who were the Doolittle Raiders raised the confidence of all Americans, civilians and military alike.

LEFT: **The deck of USS _Enterprise_ during the Battle of Midway. The carrier's Dauntless dive-bombers are being readied for flight. The Douglas Dauntless had the lowest loss ratio of any US carrier aircraft of World War II.** ABOVE: **Admiral Chester W. Nimitz had a major advantage – cryptoanalysts had broken the Japanese Navy code and knew that Midway was the target of the impending Japanese strike, as well as a likely date and a Japanese Navy order of battle. This meant he was able to ignore the Japanese attempts to draw elements of his force away.**

The Battle of Midway

The Battle of Midway was among the most significant naval battles of World War II and carrier-borne aircraft played the major role. In mid-1942, the Japanese Navy sought to draw the US Pacific Fleet into a decisive battle that would tip the balance of naval power in Japan's favour once and for all. Their plan was to seize the island of Midway, which was close enough to Pearl Harbor to be a threat, and provoke a US naval response. The Japanese Navy then planned to ambush the US Fleet as it came to defend and retake Midway.

Unfortunately for the Japanese, the US Navy codebreakers had deciphered their enemy's coded transmissions and found that a trap had been set. This gave Admiral Nimitz, US Navy Commander-in-Chief Pacific, the opportunity to best deploy his smaller forces. Four Japanese carriers steamed towards Midway while Admiral Yamamoto's group remained behind waiting to ambush the American aircraft carriers that would make their way to defend Midway. Although the United States knew what Japan had planned, the US Navy did not know the exact location of the enemy ships.

At dawn on June 4, 1942, the Japanese began their air attack on Midway but met stiff resistance from the defending fighters. This called for a second raid and by this time Vice-Admiral Nagumo's ships were coming under limited attack by Midway-based USAAF B-17 and B-26 bombers as well as SBU Vindicator dive-bombers.

By this stage, the strike aircraft still available to the Japanese (the rest were on the way back from Midway) were configured to attack the expected intervening US ships. Instead the aircraft had to have different ordnance loaded

for a repeat attack on Midway. When Japanese patrol aircraft reported American warships to the north of the island, the order was given to again change the ordnance so the target would be the newly discovered US warships. This chaotic period inevitably resulted in all manner of ordnance laying around the below-deck aircraft hangars as orders changed and the decks were emptied for the aircraft returning from Midway.

It was at this time that the US air attacks against the Japanese fleet began. Three squadrons of TBD Devastator torpedo-bombers were decimated by anti-aircraft fire and defending Zero fighters. Of the 41 aircraft that attacked, only 4 made it back. While the Japanese were congratulating themselves, another formation of SBD Dauntless bombers from _Yorktown_ and _Enterprise_ arrived unnoticed. Lieutenant Commander Clarence Wade McClusky, air-group commander of the _Enterprise_, had led 32 of the Dauntless dive-bombers in search of Japanese naval targets.

Below him suddenly appeared the _Kaga_ and _Akagi_. McClusky led his formation straight down at the carriers in a 70-degree dive. The _Kaga_ took a direct hit and its deck, full of aircraft, ordnance and fuel, erupted. A second bomb crashed through the forward aircraft elevator and exploded among the fuelled aircraft on the hangar deck. A third bomb hit a fuel bowser, which exploded and destroyed the bridge, killing the captain and other senior officers. At 17:00 hours the surviving crew were ordered to abandon ship.

The _Akagi_ took a bomb in the midship elevator, which exploded ammunition nearby while a second bomb struck the aircraft being rearmed and refuelled on the deck. The ensuing

LEFT: **Hit by a shell from the** *Yorktown* **during a torpedo run, a Nakajima 'Kate' breaks up in mid-air before dropping its deadly torpedo which can be seen falling safely away.** ABOVE: **The flight deck of USS** *Yorktown* **looking aft shortly after she was hit by two Japanese torpedoes. Men are balancing themselves on the listing deck as they prepare to abandon the carrier – one crew member is already wearing a life jacket. The crew were ordered to abandon the ship at 14:55 hours but the carrier remained afloat a day later. The** *Yorktown* **was finally sunk by Japanese torpedoes while under tow for repair assessment.** BELOW LEFT: **An artist's impression of the action during the Battle of Midway.** BELOW: *Akagi* **was a 36,500-ton aircraft carrier that began life as a battlecruiser. She was completed as one of Japan's first two large aircraft carriers in March 1927. The** *Akagi* **was flagship for the Pearl Harbor attack in December 1941 and later took part in carrier raids into the Indian Ocean area. During Midway, as**

the flagship of Admiral Nagumu, the *Akagi* **is pictured taking evasive manoeuvres while under attack by dive-bombers from the USS** *Enterprise.* **Although seriously damaged, the carrier did not sink but was scuttled by Japanese destroyer torpedoes early the following day.**

fires raged out of control and the order to abandon ship was given at 19:00 hours.

Meanwhile, the carrier *Soryu* was attacked and hit by Dauntless squadron VB-3 from the USS *Yorktown*, led by Lieutenant Commander Maxwell F. Leslie. The resulting fire on the Japanese carrier was so intense that the armoured hangar doors melted. The carrier was out of action by 10:40 hours and sank around 19:20.

The fourth Japanese carrier, *Hiryu*, shrouded in haze, was spared at that stage and launched an attack against the *Yorktown*. One Japanese bomb smashed through the ship's side and destroyed five of the carrier's boilers. A number of torpedo hits sealed the *Yorktown*'s fate and the order to abandon ship was given at 14:55. Within a couple of hours, however, a US aircraft had found the *Hiryu* and ten minutes later the *Enterprise* launched a formation of dive-bombers against the Japanese carrier. The dive-bombers flew unprotected as the fighters had to remain to defend the

American ships against air attack. Thirteen dive-bombers struck at the carrier while her pilots were in the mess. Four bombs struck in quick succession, completely destroying the flight deck and setting the hangar deck below on fire. Although no bomb penetrated deep into the ship and it was still able to steam at 30 knots after the attack, the fires could not be controlled. The *Hiryu* was abandoned by its crew in the early hours of June 5.

In just one day, four of the six carriers that had launched the devastating air attack against the US at Pearl Harbor had been destroyed. Japan also lost more than 300 aircraft and 3,000 men, including many of Imperial Japanese Navy's most experienced aircrew.

Yamamoto still had a huge battle force that could outgun the US Pacific Fleet but, without the protection of his aircraft carriers, the Japanese admiral's gamble had not paid off and he had no option but to withdraw from the fight. From then on, Japan had to fight a largely defensive war.

The growth of naval aviation

In August 1914, Britain had no aircraft carriers, so four merchant ships were quickly converted to become seaplane carriers by the addition of a seaplane hangar. In December 1914, three of the carriers, the *Empress*, *Engadine* and *Riviera* participated in a strike against Heligoland. These ships were typical of most early Royal Navy seaplane carriers, which had to stop before they could lower their aircraft into the water for take-off. On their return the aircraft were craned back onboard. These ships remained the principal carrier type in British service at the end of World War I.

During World War I, the light battlecruiser *Furious* was converted into an aircraft carrier with a small forward take-off deck, and it was on this ship that the first successful deck landing occurred when Squadron Commander Dunning landed his Sopwith Pup on August 2, 1917. Dunning tried to repeat his achievement two days later but a burst tyre caused the aircraft to fall over the side of the carrier, drowning the pioneering naval aviator. Flying an aircraft is a complex undertaking, and becomes more so when other factors are added, such as darkness, bad weather and a carrier deck that could be moving in all three planes at once – up and down, side to side and rolling. The operation of aircraft from a carrier called for the development of special flying techniques.

The experiments on the *Furious*, however, proved that safe deck operations needed a deck free of obstructions. The Italian

ABOVE: **Naval aviation presents even greater hazards than land-based aviation, and this was more so when the techniques for operating from early carrier decks were being developed. Squadron Commander E.H. Dunning pioneered deck landings on Royal Navy ships in August 1917, to prove it could be done by flying around the inconveniently positioned funnel. Sadly, during the trials his Sopwith Camel went over the side of HMS *Furious*.**

liner *Conte Rosso* was bought and converted into a 'flat top' aircraft carrier and renamed *Argus*, while *Furious* was modified to take a full-length flight deck. In July 1918, *Furious* launched six Sopwith Camels against Zeppelin sheds on what became the first-ever carrier strike.

ABOVE: **This photograph, taken on a Royal Navy carrier, illustrates many of the elements of carrier operation. A variety of aircraft types, a cramped deck, the elevator in action taking aircraft below and the deck crew anxiously watching for the next aircraft to land.**

The first US aircraft carrier, the USS *Langley*, was commissioned in 1922, while the first purpose-designed aircraft carrier was Japan's *Hosho* of 1925. France's first aircraft carrier, *Béarn*, entered service in 1927. By 1939, Britain had six aircraft carriers in service and by 1941 the USA had eight aircraft carriers. Meanwhile, Japan had ten aircraft carriers.

Aircraft take off from a carrier to the bow, into the wind, and land from the stern. Carriers steam at speed into the wind during take-off to increase the wind speed over the deck, leading to more lift for the aircraft taking off.

Pilots making an approach would rely on the skill of a 'batsman' or landing signal officer to control the plane's landing approach. 'Bats' visually gauged the approaching aircraft's speed, altitude and attitude and relayed the information and corrections to the pilot using coloured paddles like ping-pong bats. When landing on a carrier, an aircraft would rely on its tailhook catching one of a number of arrester wires stretched across the deck to bring it to a stop in a shorter distance than if it was landing on a normal runway.

Into the 1950s, aircraft would land on the flight deck parallel to the ship's centreline. Aircraft already recovered would be parked at the bow end of the flight deck. A metal mesh safety barrier would then be raised behind the recovered aircraft in case the next aircraft to land missed the wires and overshot.

This problem was overcome by the later introduction of the angled deck, a British innovation introduced in the 1950s. In this configuration the runway was aligned off-centre a few degrees across the ship. Any aircraft missing the arrester cables on landing would then have the opportunity to employ maximum power to take off from an unobstructed deck and go around again as the other aircraft had left the 'runway' and parked in safety to the side.

ABOVE: **Two classic naval types in the air together. The Grumman Avenger (foreground) would never have sought out Japan's Mitsubishi Zero for combat, but often drew unwanted attention from the excellent fighter.**
BELOW: **The Grumman Wildcat (or Martlet as it was briefly known by the Royal Navy) typifies how advances in aircraft technology made carriers more potent. The unique Grumman wing-folding mechanism meant the fighter took up much less room in the hangar and on deck so more could be taken onboard.**

LEFT: **Carrier operations were and are still high-risk situations. Here a US Navy Grumman Hellcat burns following a landing accident. Incidents like this could prevent other aircraft landing or force them to head for another carrier, dry land or consider ditching. Aircraft coming in to land after combat were often low on fuel, so any delay in landing was feared.** ABOVE: **A deck crewman uses a variety of hand signals to tell the pilot what to do next, having taken the wire and landed on this carrier. An aircraft is taken below to the hangar deck on the elevator – the waiting Hellcat is next.**

Seaplanes and flying boats to 1945

Historians disagree over who first lifted off from water in an aircraft but it was possibly the Austrian Wilhelm Kress. His tandem-winged aircraft, powered by a 30hp engine, reportedly took off, albeit briefly, from an Austrian reservoir in October 1901. The first proper take-off from water was made by Frenchman Henri Fabre in a seaplane named *Hydravion* on March 28, 1910.

While aircraft carriers were being developed to project military might, some aircraft designers were striving to perfect those frequently overlooked naval aircraft types, seaplanes and flying boats. 'Seaplane' is an American description for any kind of aircraft designed to operate from water, although they have been developed into many forms. Flying boats have a fuselage with an underside designed like a boat – a planing hull. Typically flying boats have wing-mounted floats to stabilize the aircraft while it is on or moving through the water, although manufacturers like Savoia-Marchetti produced large flying boats with twin parallel hulls and no floats. Amphibians are flying boats that also have an undercarriage so can operate from land or water – some versions of the Catalina were built this way.

Floatplanes were traditionally designed aircraft, often land-based designs, mounted on floating pontoons. Floatplanes were among the most pioneering of early aircraft, partly because so many record-breaking flights were made over great expanses of water and the ability to put down on water increased the pilot's chances of survival in an emergency such as a fuel shortage.

The cutting-edge reputation of floatplanes was helped in no small way by the famous Schneider Trophy races that took place between 1913 and 1931. The competition was intended

TOP: **The Farman Aviation Works founded and run by brothers Henry and Maurice Farman developed this floatplane version of their MF 11 Shorthorn. It was used for reconnaissance, bombing and training roles. This machine is pictured at Felixstowe.** ABOVE: **Fabre's Hydravion was a seaplane with a fuselage structure of two beams that carried unequal span biplane surfaces with a tailplane at the forward end and a monoplane wing at the rear. The Gnome rotary engine drove a pusher propeller mounted at the rear of the upper fuselage beam.**

to encourage technical advances in aviation but gradually became a contest of speed over a measured course. The Schneider Trophy significantly accelerated aircraft design, particularly in aerodynamics and engine development. It was a floatplane winner of the Schneider, the Supermarine S.6B, that led directly to the development of the Spitfire.

The streamlined advanced aircraft that took part and their low drag, liquid-cooled engines also influenced the designs of the North American P-51 Mustang and the Italian Macchi C.202 Folgore. Although floatplane versions of famous fighters such as the Mitsubishi Zero and the Spitfire were built during World War II, these developments were usually abandoned in favour of carrier-borne combat aircraft. It was, however, in the time before the arrival into service of helicopters that many warships carried their own floatplanes for reconnaissance. The Nakajima E8N2 was a short-range reconnaissance floatplane that could be launched from a catapult. Small flying boats were, however, also used in this way – the Supermarine Walrus was an air sea rescue/spotter amphibian that was carried on some Royal Navy cruisers during World War II. It 'lived' on the warship's deck with its wings folded to save space and then when required would be lowered by a deck crane into the sea. At the end of its sortie the process would be reversed.

Flying boats, however, were barely influenced by the developments driven by the Schneider Trophy. By their nature, these aircraft were built for range and endurance and generally grew larger and heavier until, like the dinosaurs some of the later, larger ones resembled, they became extinct. Germany's Blohm und Voss Bv 238 was the largest built by the country and was designed for long-range reconnaissance duties. With a wing span of over 60m/197ft it was powered by no less than six engines but only one prototype, weighing more than 80,000kg/176,000lb was built. Britain's largest military flying boat was the Short Shetland of which only two prototypes were built and flown towards the end of World War II. Although these aircraft were at the evolutionary extreme for piston engine-powered flying boats, they had been preceded by many types that were extraordinarily successful such as the Short Sunderland and Kawanishi H8K2.

ABOVE: **The Grumman Duck with its distinctive streamlined integral float served throughout World War II in a variety of roles and was used by the US Navy, Coast Guard and Marine Corps. The type is known to have attacked German U-boats as well as serving in the coastal patrol and reconnaissance roles.**
BELOW: **The Blackburn Shark was a versatile torpedo-bomber that could be equipped with an undercarriage or floats.**

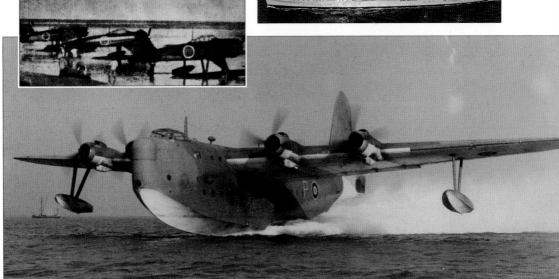

TOP: **The Nakajima A6M2-N 'Rufe' was a floatplane development of the famous A6M Zero intended for use in support of amphibious operations.**
ABOVE: **The Short Shetland carried on the Short's tradition of large flying boats established with the C-class boats that became the Sunderland. The Shetland, impressive as it was, was not needed in the post-war world when new large flying boats were considered to be surplus to requirements.**

An A–Z of Naval Aircraft in World Wars I and II

The marriage of military aviation and sea power was a potent mix, perhaps best demonstrated by the devastating attack carried out on Pearl Harbor in December 1941 by Japanese aircraft operating from aircraft carriers. Without the carriers and the specialized aircraft that operated from the carriers, the Japanese could never have struck Pearl Harbor. These floating airfields carried fighters for defence and for attacking enemy aircraft, but could also carry purpose-designed attack aircraft such as dive-bombers that, in the hands of skilled pilots, could destroy enormous warships. The same was true of the torpedo-bomber, which could launch devastating attacks on surface vessels.

Prior to World War II, naval aircraft tended to be the poor relations of the high-performance land-based types. As the opposing sides squared up to fight in World War II, there was no room for second best in the battles that were fought, sometimes thousands of miles from major land masses. Modifications to aircraft like the Spitfire and Hurricane were a useful stopgap but these aircraft were in a different league to the tough, purpose-designed naval aircraft like the Grumman Hellcat that proved to be real war winners.

LEFT: **Two classic Grumman purpose-designed naval fighters flying in formation – the Bearcat (closest) and the Hellcat. The 'cat' series continued to the F-14 Tomcat into the 2000s.**

Aichi D3A

This two-seat low-wing monoplane dive-bomber, codenamed 'Val' by the Allies, came to prominence on December 7, 1941, during the attack on Pearl Harbor. When the Japanese naval task force launched its first wave of 183 aircraft from six aircraft carriers to attack Pearl Harbor's Battleship Row and other US Navy installations on the Hawaiian island of Oahu, among them were 51 Aichi D3As. This first wave of the attack was led by a formation of D3As, which became the first Japanese aircraft to drop bombs on American targets during World War II. One of the D3As' victims during the attack was the American Pacific Fleet flagship USS *Pennsylvania*. In all, 129 Aichi D3A aircraft were used as part of the Japanese Pearl Harbor task force.

After the attack and despite its relative obsolescence, the D3A took part in all major Japanese carrier operations

ABOVE: **In mid-1936 the Imperial Japanese Navy issued a specification for a monoplane carrier-based dive-bomber to replace the D1A then in service. Aichi, Nakajima and Mitsubishi all submitted designs.**

in the first ten months of the war. Prior to the 'Day of Infamy' at Pearl Harbor, the type had only seen limited action from land bases in China and Indochina.

The D3A was designed to replace the Aichi D1A2 Navy Type 96 Carrier Bomber and featured a fixed landing gear to eliminate extra weight as well as the maintenance demands of a retractable undercarriage. The outer 1.83m/6ft sections of the wing hinged up to save space during carrier stowage.

The type had first flown in January 1938, and between December 1939 and August 1945 the Aichi company built a total of 1,495 aircraft in two main variants.

ABOVE: **Preparing to unleash the 'Day of Infamy', Aichi D3A1 'Val' dive-bombers get ready to take off from a Japanese aircraft carrier during the morning of December 7, 1941, to attack Pearl Harbor.**

ABOVE: **US Navy personnel prepare to remove a D3A that crashed during the attack on Pearl Harbor. The Japanese only lost 29 aircraft during the attack, but United States military losses were huge.**

LEFT: **A crashed D3A being craned on to a salvage barge following the Pearl Harbor attack.**
BELOW: **This stamp shows the D3A1's fixed undercarriage fitted with streamlined fairings to reduce the drag. Weight saving and simplification were achieved at the expense of performance.**

The Type D3A1 entered service with the Imperial Japanese Navy in 1940. The production D3A1 featured a 1,000hp Mitsubishi Kinsei 43 or 1,070hp Kinsei 44 engine. A large dorsal fin was installed to correct directional stability problems and the aircraft was equipped with only two forward-firing 7.7mm Type 97 machine-guns and one flexible rear-firing 7.7mm Type 92 machine-gun. Typical bomb load was a single 250kg/551lb bomb carried under the fuselage. Two additional 60kg/132lb bombs could be carried on wing racks beneath each wing outboard of the dive brakes.

The D3A2, the main production version, had the more powerful 1,300hp Kinsei engine and increased fuel capacity of 1,079 litres/237 gallons which gave an increased range of 1,472km/915 miles. This version can be identified by the addition of a longer rear canopy section. Some 1,016 examples were built by the time it was considered obsolete at the end of 1942. Nevertheless, in April 1942, during attacks on the British cruisers HMS *Cornwall* and HMS *Dorsetshire* in the Indian Ocean, D3As are known to have released over 82 per cent of their ordnance on target. During this action, the British carrier *Hermes* also sank following attacks by 'Vals' – the only Royal Navy carrier lost to enemy air attack during World War II.

Commonwealth of Dominica **$2**

AICHI D3AI TYPE 99 'VAL'

The arrival of the faster Yokosuka Suisei relegated the D3A2s to land-based units and to smaller carriers too short for the Suisei's higher landing speed.

Over the following years, many 'Vals' were used as training aircraft but as the war progressed and the Americans moved closer to the Japanese mainland, most of the remaining aircraft were used in desperate kamikaze suicide attacks against US naval ships at Leyte and Okinawa.

ABOVE: **The 'Val' was credited with dive-bombing and sinking the only Royal Navy carrier lost during World War II. Inevitably, the type was also used for kamikaze attacks as the Japanese position worsened.**

Aichi D3A1 'Val'

First flight: January 1938
Power: One Mitsubishi 1,070hp Kinsei 44 radial piston engine
Armament: Two 7.7mm machine-guns in upper forward fuselage plus one in rear cockpit; external bomb load of 370kg/816lb
Size: Wingspan – 14.37m/47ft 2in
Length – 10.20m/33ft 5in
Height – 3.80m/12ft 7in
Wing area – 34.9m²/376sq ft
Weights: Empty – 2,408kg/5,309lb
Maximum take-off – 3,650kg/8,047lb
Performance: Maximum speed – 385kph/239mph
Service ceiling – 9,300m/30,510ft
Range – 1,470km/913 miles
Climb – 3,000m/9,845ft in 6 minutes

Arado Ar 196

From 1933, the German Navy (*Kriegsmarine*) operated shipborne reconnaissance aircraft – catapult launched in the harshest conditions and recovered by crane, the aircraft were carried by all major warships, including battleships. By 1936 the types in use were considered obsolete and, following a competition, Arado's twin-float Ar 196 was chosen to be the replacement aircraft in *Kriegsmarine* service. Following further testing and development, the Ar 196A-1 entered service in June 1939. Warships would launch the aircraft to scout ahead looking for danger or targets of opportunity.

Tirpitz and *Bismarck* carried six aircraft each while the *Scharnhorst* and *Gneisnau* had four. Heavy cruisers carried

ABOVE: **As well as its shipborne service, the Arado Ar 196 also served with coastal reconnaissance units. This Ar 196A-5 served in the eastern Mediterranean and Aegean Seas in 1943.** BELOW LEFT: **The type was the standard equipment of Germany's capital ships – the *Tirpitz* and *Bismarck* each carried six examples of the aircraft. The aircraft were catapulted off a launch rail when required and then hoisted back on deck on their return.**

three while smaller battleships and cruisers had two. The first operational cruise for two of these early aircraft was aboard the pocket battleship *Admiral Graf Spee* when it sailed for the South Atlantic in August 1939. The Arados took the warship's 'eyes' well over the horizon to look for prospective targets and located the majority of the ship's 11 British victims. During the Battle of the River Plate in December 1939, both of the *Spee*'s aircraft were destroyed on the ship's deck by British gunfire.

However, as well as equipping the fleet, the type also served widely with shore units on coastal reconnaissance duties. The Ar 196A-2 was designed to operate from shore bases looking for enemy shipping, although forward-firing cannon fitted within the wings gave the Arado a powerful punch against enemy aircraft as well as surface vessels. In addition the type had a 7.9mm forward-firing machine-gun in the fuselage nose and up to two 7.9mm flexible guns in the rear cockpit. A 50kg/110lb bomb could also be carried under each wing. On May 5, 1940, two Ar 196s operating from a shorebase in Denmark spotted Royal Navy submarine HMS *Seal*, damaged by a mine it was trying to lay. After repeated attacks by the two floatplanes the submarine, so damaged it was unable to dive, surrendered to one of the floatplanes as it landed next to it.

Other land-based Ar 196s operating along the French coast of the Bay of Biscay successfully intercepted RAF Whitley bombers attacking German U-boats sailing to and from their protective pens.

Each of the aircraft's two floats contained a 300-litre/ 66-gallon fuel tank while the aircraft's wings could be folded manually to the rear. A continuous greenhouse-style canopy covered the pilot and observer's positions – the latter crewmember was unable to completely close his section of canopy, ensuring the rear cockpit armament was always at readiness. Visibility was good from the cockpit and the type, easy to handle both in the air and on water, proved popular with its crews. In all, 541 Ar 196s were built (of which 526 were production models) before production ended in August 1944. About 100 examples were built at SNCA and Fokker plants in France and Holland respectively. The Arado Ar 196 was the last fighting floatplane built in Europe.

Only three Ar 196 floatplanes survive. A machine preserved in Bulgaria is one of twelve the Bulgarian air force operated from coastal bases during World War II. Romania was the only other customer for the type. Two other aircraft, captured by the Allies when the battlecruiser *Prinz Eugen* surrendered at Copenhagen, are preserved in the US Naval Aviation Museum and the National Air and Space Museum in the USA.

ABOVE LEFT AND ABOVE: **Although the aircraft's basic design was decided early on, there was uncertainty regarding the best arrangement of floats. Accordingly prototypes were built using both single and twin floats, the single-float models pictured here having two smaller outrigger floats for stability. Some single-float aircraft did see limited service even though evaluation showed the twin-float configuration to be best.** BELOW: **The float rudders on the twin-float production model aided manoeuvring on the water and are clearly visible in this air-to-air study. The long floats also each contained a 300-litre/66-gallon fuel tank.**

ABOVE: **The Ar 196 was the last combat floatplane to be built in Europe, and the type also saw service with the Bulgarian and Romanian air forces through to mid-1944. The aircraft's wings were all metal but with fabric-covered control surfaces.**

Arado Ar 196A-3

First flight: Summer 1937 (prototype)
Power: One BMW 960hp 312K radial engine
Armament: Two 20mm cannon in outer wings, one fixed forward-firing 7.92mm machine-gun, one 7.92mm machine-gun aimed by observer and two 50kg/110lb bombs under wings
Size: Wingspan – 12.44m/40ft 10in
    Length – 10.96m/35ft 11in
    Height – 4.44m/14ft 7in
    Wing area – 28.3m²/305sq ft
Weights: Empty – 2,572kg/5,670lb
    Maximum take-off – 3,303kg/7,282lb
Performance: Maximum speed – 312kph/194mph
    Service ceiling – 7,000m/22,965ft
    Range – 800km/497 miles
    Climb – 414m/1,358ft per minute

LEFT: **Designed by Major F.A. Bumpus, the Blackburn Baffin was a conventional two-seat single-bay biplane torpedo-bomber of mixed metal and wood construction with fabric covering.**

Blackburn Baffin

First flight: September 30, 1932
Power: One Bristol 565hp Pegasus IM3 radial engine
Armament: One fixed 0.303in forward-firing Vickers machine-gun, one 0.303in Lewis machine-gun in rear cockpit and up to 907kg/2,000lb of bombs or one torpedo
Size: Wingspan – 13.88m/45ft 7in
　　　Length – 11.68m/38ft 4in
　　　Height – 3.91m/12ft 10in
　　　Wing area – 63.45m²/683sq ft
Weights: Empty – 1,444kg/3,184lb
　　　Maximum take-off – 3,452kg/7,610lb
Performance: Maximum speed – 219kph/136mph
　　　Service ceiling – 4,570m/15,000ft
　　　Range – 869km/540 miles
　　　Climb – 146m/480ft per minute

Blackburn Baffin

The prototype Baffin, originally known as the Ripon V, differed sufficiently from the earlier Ripon marks to warrant a new name. Inspired by the local installation of radial engines in Finnish-built Ripons, Fairey pursued their own radial-engined version as a private venture. The successful tests of the two-seat torpedo-bomber prototype led not just to a new name but also to an order

from the Fleet Air Arm who began replacing early mark Ripons with Baffins from January 1934. The first unit to re-equip was No.812 Squadron on HMS *Glorious*. Although only 29 aircraft were built from new as Baffins, over 60 more Ripons were 'upgraded' to Baffin standard by the installation of the Bristol Pegasus I.M3 radial engine. Upgrade is something of a misnomer as the

performance was little improved over that of the Ripon and consequently the type was considered obsolete by 1937. In that year, New Zealand bought 29 of the surplus Baffins for coastal defence duties, some of them serving as late as 1941.

Blackburn Iris

The Iris was the first flying boat produced by the Yorkshire-based Blackburn Aeroplane and Motor Co Ltd. It was designed in response to a specification for an RAF long-range reconnaissance aircraft. June 19, 1926, saw the first flight of this five-man three-engined wooden biplane flying boat; its distinctive biplane tail had an elevator on the upper plane and three rudders. The two pilots sat side by side in an open

cockpit while their fellow crew also sat in open cockpits to their rear.

Following evaluation, the prototype (the Iris I) was returned to Blackburn where an all-metal hull was fitted together with more powerful engines – the aircraft was then redesignated Iris II.

The aircraft's ruggedness is best demonstrated by the fact that on September 28, 1928, the Under Secretary of State for Air, Sir Philip Sassoon, embarked on a 15,929km/9,900-mile flight in a Blackburn Iris from Felixstowe to Karachi and back, to inspect Royal

Air Force units in Malta, Egypt and Iraq. The aircraft returned to Britain on November 14, 1928.

Three improved production Iris IIIs entered RAF squadron service in 1930, becoming the largest type in the inventory. These were re-engined and became Iris IVs.

Blackburn Iris

First flight: June 19, 1926
Power: Three Rolls-Royce 570hp Condor IIIB piston engines
Armament: Three 0.303in machine-guns (nose, mid-fuselage and tail) plus up to 907kg/2,000lb of bombs
Size: Wingspan – 29.57m/97ft
　　　Length – 20.54m/67ft 5in
　　　Height – 7.77m/25ft 6in
　　　Wing area – 207.07m²/2,229sq ft
Weights: Empty – 8,640kg/19,048lb
　　　Maximum take-off – 13,376kg/29,489lb
Performance: Maximum speed – 190kph/118mph
　　　Service ceiling – 3,230m/10,600ft
　　　Range – 1,287km/800 miles
　　　Climb – 184m/603ft per minute

LEFT: **Looking as much boat as aircraft, the Blackburn Iris was a sturdy flying machine that served in the Royal Air Force from 1930–34.**

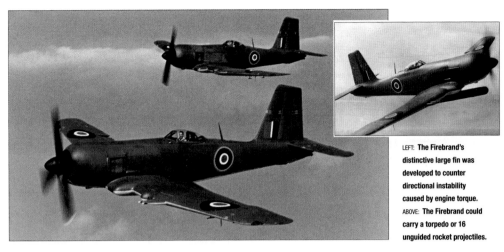

LEFT: **The Firebrand's distinctive large fin was developed to counter directional instability caused by engine torque.**
ABOVE: **The Firebrand could carry a torpedo or 16 unguided rocket projectiles.**

Blackburn Firebrand

Outline designs for what became the Firebrand were first produced in response to a 1939 Admiralty requirement for a single-seat four-gun carrier-borne aircraft to replace the Gladiator, Fulmar and Skua. Designed around the Napier Sabre III 24-cylinder engine, the first flight of the first of three Firebrand prototypes took place on February 27, 1942. Nine production examples were completed as Firebrand F.1s while the second prototype was undergoing carrier trials on HMS *Illustrious*. The second prototype was modified with a wider wing centre section to improve the type's torpedo-carrying ability, leading to the production of 12 Firebrand TF.IIs. These aircraft served with trials unit No.708 Squadron, the only Fleet Air Arm unit to receive the type during World War II.

The Sabre engine was also used to power the Hawker Typhoon fighter and

this type was given priority for the engines. Consequently, a new powerplant was needed for the Firebrand and the Bristol Centaurus was chosen. This required some changes to the airframe to accommodate the new engine, and this version was designated the Firebrand TF.III. It had its first flight on December 21, 1943.

The new engine produced more torque than the Sabre and required an enlarged fin and rudder to counteract the resultant directional instability. The TF.III was considered unsuitable for carrier operations so the 27 production examples were confined to land duties while the improved TF.4 was developed.

The first Firebrand variant to see mass production, 102 examples of these TF.4 were built, and first entered FAA service in September 1945. The ultimate production Firebrand was the TF.5, featuring minor aerodynamic improvements.

The Firebrand was a classic compromise aircraft – a torpedo-fighter that excelled neither as a fighter nor torpedo-carrier. By the time the type's many faults were rectified, much more capable aircraft were available. Despite this, the type lumbered on in Royal Navy service until 1953.

The Firebrand was unusual in that there was an extra airspeed gauge mounted outside the cockpit so that during landing the pilot would not have to look down into the cockpit to take instrument readings – which is a clue to the poor low-speed handling characteristics of the type.

Blackburn Firebrand TF.5

First flight: February 27, 1942
Power: One Bristol 2,520hp Centaurus IX radial piston engine
Armament: Four 20mm cannon, plus one torpedo or sixteen 27kg/60lb rockets
Size: Wingspan – 15.63m/51ft 4in
Length – 11.81m/38ft 9in
Height – 4.04m/13ft 3in
Wing area – 35.58m²/383sq ft
Weights: Empty – 5,368kg/11,835lb
Maximum take-off – 7,938kg/17,500lb
Performance: Maximum speed – 547kph/340mph
Service ceiling – 8,685m/28,500ft
Range – 1,191km/740 miles
Climb – 701m/2,300ft per minute

LEFT: **One of the early Sabre-engined Blackburn Firebrands. Its poor fighter performance led to its unfortunate development as a torpedo-fighter.**

Blackburn Perth

First flight: October 11, 1933
Power: Three Rolls-Royce 825hp Buzzard IIMS in-line piston engines
Armament: One 37mm automatic gun, three 0.303in machine-guns in nose, mid-fuselage and tail positions plus a bomb load of up to 907kg/2,000lb
Size: Wingspan – 29.57m/97ft
　　　 Length – 21.34m/70ft
　　　 Height – 8.06m/26ft 6in
　　　 Wing area – 233.27m²/2,511sq ft
Weights: Empty – 9,492kg/20,927lb
　　　 Maximum take-off –17,237kg/38,000lb
Performance: Maximum speed – 212kph/132mph
　　　 Service ceiling – 3,505m/11,500ft
　　　 Range – 2,414km/1,500 miles
　　　 Climb – 244m/800ft per minute

Blackburn Perth

Derived from, and designed to replace, Blackburn's own Iris flying boat in service with No.209 Squadron at Mount Batten, the Perth entered service in January 1934. The Perth differed from the Iris by having an enclosed cockpit for the pilots and power provided by three Rolls-Royce Buzzard engines. The other significant difference was the Perth's primary armament – a bow-mounted 37mm automatic anti-shipping gun that could fire 0.68kg/1.5lb shells at the rate of 100 rounds per minute.

In addition to the pilot and co-pilot, the Perth's crew consisted of a navigator, wireless (radio) operator, an engineer gunner and a gunner. An interior 'cabin' included sleeping berths, a galley, mess, radio room, and a navigation compartment complete with a chart table which emphasized the 'boat' in flying boat.

Built in small numbers for the RAF (4), the Perth served until May 1936 and has the distinction of being the largest biplane flying boat ever operated by the RAF.

Blackburn Ripon

The two-seat Blackburn Ripon with its 12-hour endurance was a carrier-borne torpedo-bomber and reconnaissance aircraft developed from Blackburn's Swift, Dart and Velos design family and devised to replace the Dart in Fleet Air Arm service. Two prototypes flew in 1928, one a landplane, the other a floatplane. The first production version, the Ripon II powered by a 570hp Lion XI engine, began to enter service in July 1929 and first equipped units on board HMS *Furious* and *Glorious*.

The Ripon IIA could carry a range of offensive loads including a torpedo, while the last production variant, the Ripon IIC, introduced aluminium and steel in the wing construction in place of wood.

UK Ripon production ended in 1932 but a single example of an export version, the Ripon IIF, was sold to Finland as a pattern aircraft. Having interchangeable wheels and float landing gear, 25 examples were produced under licence in Finland. Some of these carried out reconnaissance of Russian forces in the winter of 1939–40 while others later flew night-time anti-submarine patrols. The last Finnish machine was retired in December 1944 and one of these machines survives in a Finnish museum. Fleet Air Arm Ripons were removed from front-line service in 1935 but some served in secondary roles until the start of World War II.

Blackburn Ripon IIA

First flight: April 17, 1926 (prototype)
Power: One Napier 570hp Lion XIA in-line piston engine
Armament: One fixed forward-firing 0.303in machine-gun and one 0.303in machine-gun in rear cockpit plus up to 680kg/1,500lb bombs or one torpedo
Size: Wingspan – 13.67m/44ft 10in
　　　 Length – 11.20m/36ft 9in
　　　 Height – 3.91m/12ft 10in
　　　 Wing area – 63.45m²/683sq ft
Weights: Empty – 1,930kg/4,255lb
　　　 Maximum take-off – 3,359kg/7,405lb
Performance: Maximum speed – 203kph/126mph
　　　 Service ceiling – 3,050m/10,000ft
　　　 Range – 1,706km/1,060 miles
　　　 Climb – 155m/510ft per minute

Blackburn Skua

The Blackburn Skua was a departure for the Fleet Air Arm as it was an all-metal monoplane, which contrasted sharply with the fabric-covered biplanes that equipped the FAA for most of its history. It was also the Fleet Air Arm's first naval dive-bomber and their first carrier aircraft with flaps, a retractable undercarriage and a variable-pitch propeller. Despite these innovations, the two-seat fighter/torpedo-bomber was virtually obsolete when it entered service in August 1938.

The first Skua prototype had its maiden flight at Brough on February 9, 1937, but an order for 190 production aircraft (Skua II) had been placed months before, such was the urgency to bolster the FAA inventory as war clouds gathered in Europe.

As a fighter it was no match for contemporary enemy types but on September 26, 1939, a Skua of *Ark Royal*'s 803 Squadron shot down the first enemy aircraft of World War II, a German Do18 flying boat. Its dive-bombing capabilities were also proven early in World War II. On April 10, 1940, 16 Skuas of Nos.800 and 803 Squadrons flew from the Orkneys to Bergen harbour in the night. Arriving at dawn they bombed and sank the German cruiser *Königsberg*, the first large warship sunk by Allied forces in the war. The returning aircraft (one was lost) were virtually empty of fuel having operated at the extreme of their range.

TOP LEFT: **Early production Skuas of No.803 Squadron in pre-war paint scheme.** TOP RIGHT: **It may be hard to believe today, but the all-metal monoplane Skua was considered very advanced for its time. It was the only naval dive-bomber in British use for the first two years of the war. It was, however, soon considered obsolete when pitted against the latest German fighter types.** ABOVE: **The Blackburn Skua was the first monoplane aircraft to enter service with the Fleet Air Arm and was still the only monoplane serving with the Fleet Air Arm at the start of World War II.**

Eleven days later most of the victorious aircraft and crews were lost on an attack on Narvik. On June 13, 1940, disaster occurred when the Skuas of 800 Squadron, attempting to dive-bomb the German ship *Scharnhorst* at Trondheim, were decimated by the Messerschmitt Bf 109s of II/JG77. Occasional air combat successes followed but the Skua was removed from front-line duties in 1941 when the Fairey Fulmar entered FAA service. The type continued to serve until the war's end as a trainer and target tug. No complete Skuas are known to survive.

Blackburn Skua II

First flight: February 9, 1937
Power: One Bristol 905hp Perseus XII radial engine
Armament: Four 0.303in machine-guns in wings, one 0.303in machine-gun on flexible mount in rear cockpit plus one 227kg/500lb bomb
Size: Wingspan – 14.07m/46ft 2in
Length – 10.85m/35ft 7in
Height – 3.81m/12ft 6in
Wing area – 28.98m²/312sq ft
Weights: Empty – 2,490kg/5,290lb
Maximum take-off – 3,732kg/8,228lb
Performance: Maximum speed – 362kph/225mph
Service ceiling – 6,160m/20,200ft
Range – 1,223km/760 miles
Climb – 482m/1,580ft per minute

Blohm und Voss Bv 138

The Blohm und Voss Bv 138 was named *Seedrache* (Sea Dragon) but was unofficially referred to as 'the flying clog' by its crews. The type was the wartime Luftwaffe's principal long-range maritime reconnaissance aircraft, often flying for hours far out over the sea in search of Allied convoys and shipping. The Bv 138 served in the Atlantic, Arctic, Bay of Biscay, Mediterranean, Baltic and Black Sea equipping a total of around 20 squadrons. Fully loaded it could fly over

ABOVE: **The Bv 138A-1 exhibits an impressive rotation from the water. This was an early example of the revised design rectifying the shortcomings of the Ha 138 prototype and featured an enlarged hull, as well as bigger fins and tail booms and a bow turret.** BELOW LEFT: **This study shows the relative positions of two of the aircraft's powerplants. Note the four propellers of the centre engine and the three blades of the engine to the left.**

4,000km/2,485 miles and stay aloft for 16 hours but its range could be increased further by the use of RATO packs (rocket assisted take-off) or when launched by catapult from seaplane tenders. The aircraft could land on the sea close by the tenders, be refuelled and then take off from the water again or be craned on to the tender and then catapult-launched.

Following a lengthy development period the prototype, the Ha 138V1 (registered as D-ARAK) made its first flight on July 15, 1937 – this was one of the earliest aircraft designs to emanate from Hamburger Flugzeugbau GMBH, the aircraft subsidiary of shipbuilders Blohm und Voss. Instabilities and design flaws called for a redesign which led to the Bv 138A-1 with an improved hull which set the form of the production versions that followed.

The Bv 138 was unusual as it was powered by three engines – one was mounted high above the aircraft's centreline driving a four-bladed propeller while one engine on each wing drove three-bladed propellers. Equally unusual was the aircraft's twin boom tail unit.

Although the Bv 138 could carry a small bombload or depth-charges, most operations were purely reconnaissance. For self-defence the Bv 138 was equipped with gun turrets at the bow and the stern of the fuselage, as well as behind the central engine. Although different versions of the aircraft carried various armament, the standard included two 20mm cannon and four machine-guns – the type was credited with the destruction of an RAF Catalina and a Blenheim. As the Bv 138 could absorb a lot of battle damage and the diesel fuel rarely ignited when hit by enemy fire, the type was generally well liked by its crews. It could carry 500kg/1,102lb of bombs or depth charges or, in place of these, up to ten infantry troops and all of their associated equipment.

There were three principal versions. The Bv 138A-1 was the first production version and entered service in April 1940. Twenty-five were built and the type is known to have flown reconnaissance missions during the German invasion of Norway in 1940. The Bv 138B-1, of which 24 examples were produced, entered service in December 1940 and introduced a reinforced hull and floats as well as improved engines and armament.

The Bv 138C-1 had structural strengthening and improved armament. The standard service model of which 227 were built, the Bv 138C-1, began to enter service in March 1941. Most were equipped with catapult points for operation from seaplane tenders and some were equipped with a modified fuel filter to remove possible pollutants when refuelling from U-boats. Some C-1s were also equipped with the FuG 200 *Hohentwiel* or FuG 213 *Lichtenstein S* radars which made the task of searching out enemy ships and submarines somewhat easier. Of the 227 Bv 138C-1s that were built, 164 were equipped with bomb racks, which doubled the offensive payload of the earlier versions.

Some Bv 138s were later converted for the mine-sweeping role – the Bv 138 MS variant with all weaponry removed carried a large degaussing 'hoop' with a diameter the same as the aircraft's length to explode magnetic mines at sea. In total, 297 Bv 138s were built between 1938 and 1943.

ABOVE: **With a 27m/89ft wingspan and weighing in at over 14,700kg/ 32,408lb, the Bv 138 was a large aircraft to be catapulted, but this was a fuel-saving option, as was rocket-assisted take-off.** BELOW: **A good study of a Bv 138** *Seedrache* **(Sea Dragon) showing the hull and bow turret that housed a 20mm MG 151 cannon. Note the Blohm und Voss manufacturer's logo painted on the starboard side of the flying boat's nose.**

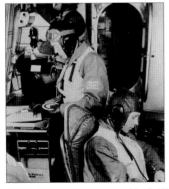

ABOVE: **Excellent study of the crew at work in a Bv 138. The** *oberleutnant* **at the centre was this aircraft's commander – note the rank patch on his left arm with the two pairs of wings and the white bar. The Bv 138** *Seedrache* **(Sea Dragon) was unofficially referred to as 'the flying clog' by its crews.**
ABOVE RIGHT: **The commander (with the lifejacket) of a moored Bv 138 flying boat reports to his squadron commander after returning from a flight.**

Blohm und Voss
Bv 138C-1

First flight: July 15, 1937 (prototype)
Power: Three Junkers 880hp Jumo 205D diesel piston engines
Armament: Two MG 151 20mm cannon, three MG 15 7.92mm machine-guns, one MG 131 13mm machine-gun plus up to 600kg/1,324lb of bombs or depth charges
Size: Wingspan – 27m/88ft 7in
　　　 Length – 19.9m/65ft 3in
　　　 Height – 6.6m/21ft 7in
　　　 Wing area – 111.9m^2/1205sq ft
Weights: Empty – 8,100kg/17,860lb
　　　 Maximum take-off – 14,700kg/32,413lb
Performance: Maximum speed – 275kph/171mph
　　　 Ceiling – 5,000m/16,400ft
　　　 Range – 5,000km/3,105 miles
　　　 Climb – 220m/722ft per minute

LEFT: The massive Blohm und Voss Bv 222 was vulnerable to attacks from fighters, and two of the 12 built were shot down.

Blohm und Voss Bv 222C

First flight: September 7, 1940
Power: Six Junkers 1,000hp Jumo 207C diesel engines
Armament: Three 20mm cannon in forward and two overwing turret positions
Size: Wingspan – 46m/150ft 11in
Length – 37m/121ft 5in
Height – 10.9m/35ft 9in
Wing area – 255m²/2,745sq ft
Weights: Empty – 30,650kg/67,572lb
Maximum take-off – 49,000kg/108,027lb
Performance: Maximum speed – 390kph/ 242mph
Service ceiling – 7,300m/23,950ft
Range – 6,095km/3,787 miles
Climb – 6,000m/19,685ft in 52 minutes

Blohm und Voss Bv 222

The Bv 222 Wiking (Viking) was the largest production military flying boat of World War II. At 46m/150ft 11in, the six-engined giant had a wingspan greater than that of the Boeing B-29 as well as flying boat rivals the Short Sunderland and Kawanishi H8K. The BV 222 was designed to meet a Deutsche Lufthansa requirement for a long-range passenger transport for their North and South Atlantic routes but, like so many German 'civil' aircraft of the time, its military applications and potential were clear to the Luftwaffe too. The unobstructed

interior floor area, due to bulkheads being kept below that level, was both useful for freight and was passenger friendly – the wings' tubular main spar contained fuel and oil tanks.

Construction of the first example, the Bv 222 V1 (registration D-ANTE) began in January 1938, but it was not until September 7, 1940, that the first prototype, flown by *Flugkapitan* Helmut Wasa Rodig, took to the air.

The first Luftwaffe Bv 222 operation using the prototype, by now fitted with larger freight doors, was flown between

Hamburg and Kirkenes, Norway, on July 10, 1941. Defended only by escorting Messerschmitt Bf 110 fighters, the Bv 222 V1, still flown by a civilian crew, began to fly regular supply missions across the Mediterranean to the *Afrika Korps* in North Africa. It was then transferred to the Mediterranean theatre. Only 12 were built.

LEFT: The sturdy and reliable Boeing biplane matched low weight with a great engine, and was one of the most widely used American aircraft of the inter-war years.

Boeing F4B-4/P-12E

First flight: June 25, 1928 (Boeing Model 83 prototype)
Power: Pratt & Whitney 550hp R-1340-16 Wasp 9-cylinder radial engine
Armament: Two fixed forward-firing 0.3in machine-guns
Size: Wingspan – 9.14m/30ft
Length – 6.12m/20ft 1in
Height – 2.84m/9ft 4in
Wing area – 21.13m²/228sq ft
Weights: Empty – 1,068kg/2,354lb
Max loaded – 1,638kg/3,611lb
Performance: Maximum speed – 303kph/188mph
Ceiling – 8,200m/26,900ft
Range – 595km/370 miles
Climb – 1,525m/5,000ft in 2 minutes, 42 seconds

Boeing F4B/P-12

Boeing developed the F4B as a private venture as a possible replacement for the US Navy's Boeing F2B and F3B fighters. Their new aircraft was smaller and lighter than the earlier Boeing machines but retained the Wasp engine of the F3B and included some design changes. Together this resulted in

improved performance which impressed the US Navy who then ordered the F4B in great quantities. Later, the US Army followed suit, giving the aircraft the designation P-12. Both the United States Navy and Army utilized a host of different variants (F4B-1, F4B-2, F4B-3, F4B-4 and P-12, P-12B, P-12C, P-12D, P-12E

and P-12F respectively) some of which served early in World War II. Though obsolete, some were hastily brought back into front-line service for air defence for a short period in the high state of alert following Pearl Harbor.

Brazil was the only major customer for the type outside the US.

Brewster F2A Buffalo

Having made carriages since 1810, in 1935 the Brewster Company decided to diversify and branched out into the aviation business. Some of the pilots who later had to go to war in this stubby fighter wished Brewster had stayed in the carriage business!

The F2A was designed to meet a US Navy specification for a carrier-based monoplane and was awarded the contract making it the Navy's first monoplane fighter. Of the 54 ordered only 11 made it into service, the rest being sold to Finland. Further contracts from the US Navy brought the F2A-2 and the more heavily armed and armoured F2A-3 into service. US Marine Corps aviators used the Buffalo to the best of their ability in the first Battle of Midway when 13 out of 19 were destroyed. This was the end of the type's US forces' use

as a front-line carrier-borne fighter as it was relegated to training duties.

Further orders placed by Britain (where the F2A was named Buffalo by the RAF and then found to be inadequate for the war in Europe) and the Netherlands East Indies brought more Buffaloes to the war in the Far East where they were thoroughly outclassed by the Japanese fighters. The aircraft's failure was due to its poor manoeuvrability, heavy weight and basic instability. In spite of this, by the time of the fall of Singapore in February 1942, RAF Buffaloes had destroyed 30 Japanese aircraft in the air, which says more about the skill and bravery of those RAF pilots than the design of the Buffalo.

Only in Finland did the Buffalo manage to hold its own when, for three years from mid-1941 until September

ABOVE: **Rejected in its early form by the US Navy despite being their first monoplane, the Buffalo was then tried by the RAF who found it to be unusable in the European theatre. Only in the Far East and Finland did the type have any measure of success.**

BELOW: **After only nine years in the business, Brewster gave up making aircraft in mid-1944.**

1944, it successfully opposed Soviet forces and then German forces until the end of the war.

LEFT: **The Brewster design that became the lacklustre Buffalo did, however, beat the Grumman XF4F1 (which led to the Wildcat) to the US Navy contract.**

Brewster F2A-3 Buffalo

First flight: December 1937

Power: Wright 1,200hp R-1820-40 Cyclone radial piston engine

Armament: Four fixed forward-firing 0.5in machine-guns

Size: Wingspan – 10.67m/35ft
Length – 8.03m/26ft 4in
Height – 3.68m/12ft 1in
Wing area – 19.41m²/209sq ft

Weights: Empty – 2,146kg/4,732lb
Maximum take-off – 3,247kg/7,159lb

Performance: Maximum speed – 517kph/321mph
Ceiling – 10,120m/33,200ft
Range – 1,553km/965 miles
Climb – 935m/3,070ft per minute

Consolidated PBY-5A Catalina

Few World War II military flying boats remain in the air today but the Catalina is a notable exception with a number still flying almost eight decades after the type was conceived. In February 1928, Consolidated received a contract for a prototype flying boat from the US Navy. The aircraft was designated XPY-1 and was unusually designed for installations of either two or three engines. It was, however, the initial configuration with two powerplants that was to ultimately develop into the most outstanding monoplane flying boat of the 1930s, the PBY Catalina.

The contract for the construction of the PBY prototype was issued to the Consolidated Aircraft Corporation in October 1933 and the aircraft flew for the first time in March 1935. Aircraft started to be delivered to the United States Navy's Patrol Squadrons in October 1936. As part of a training

TOP: **The PBY was a manifestation of many years of flying boat building experience by Consolidated. The Catalina was produced in greater numbers than any other flying boat of World War II and the type was serving with 21 USN Patrol Squadrons at the outbreak of the war.** ABOVE: **The Royal Air Force were aware of the PBY from the outset and evaluated an example at the Marine Aircraft Experimental Establishment, Felixstowe, in July 1939.**

exercise but most importantly to also demonstrate the aircraft's long-range endurance capabilities, Patrol Squadron VP-3 flew a non-stop round trip from San Diego, California, to the Panama Canal Zone in 27 hours and 58 minutes, covering a distance of 5,297km/3,292 miles.

The PB1s were powered by 850hp Pratt & Whitney R-1830-64 engines but in 1937 the engines were upgraded to 1,000hp and 50 aircraft were ordered with the designation PB-2. The third variant, the PB-3, was delivered to the Soviet Union in 1938 along with a manufacturing licence. The Soviet PB-3 was powered by two Russian-built 950hp M87 engines and designated GST. The PB-4 variant also appeared in 1938 with large mid-fuselage blister observation and gun positions.

In April 1939, the US Navy ordered a prototype amphibious version which was capable of landing on water or land (for

ABOVE: **This study gives an excellent view of the boat's two-stepped hull. Note the undercarriage wheel lying flush with the side of the fuselage and the large glazed blister forward of the tail.**

which it was fitted with an undercarriage that retracted into the fuselage) and was designated XPBY-5A. After service evaluation tests, orders were placed by the US Navy, with whom the type entered service in late 1936. Twenty-one USN Patrol Squadrons were equipped with PBYs when the USA entered World War II in December 1941.

The Royal Air Force had already shown interest in the type, aware of the gathering war clouds in Europe and the need to patrol British waters far from land. One aircraft was flown over from the US for RAF evaluation and as soon as war was declared, 30 examples of the amphibious version were ordered. These were delivered to the RAF in early 1941 and were in service almost immediately, named Catalina by the British – the US Navy also adopted the name Catalina in 1942. On a patrol on May 26, 1941, a Catalina of No.209 Squadron operating from Castle Archdale in Northern Ireland spotted the German battleship *Bismarck* after Royal Navy ships had lost the enemy ship.

Six hundred and fifty Catalinas were operated by the RAF and many served in the Atlantic. Two Royal Air Force Catalina pilots who operated in the Atlantic were awarded the Victoria Cross for gallant attacks on German submarines in the open sea. British 'Cats' also operated in Ceylon and Madagascar patrolling the Indian Ocean, while aircraft operating from Gibraltar were on station for the 1942 Allied landings in North Africa. The last U-boat sunk by RAF Coastal Command was destroyed by a No.210 Squadron Catalina on May 7, 1945.

The PBY-5A variant was used widely during World War II by a number of countries. Canadian-built versions of the flying boat were also produced and were known as Cansos in Royal Canadian Air Force service. Further development of the Catalina led to the fitting of more powerful 1,200hp engines, revised armament and search radar equipment. By the end of

ABOVE: **The Catalina entered RAF service in early 1941 operating from bases in Northern Ireland. Royal Air Force Catalinas sank 196 German U-boats during World War II, the last of them in May 1945. BELOW: In one of its elements, the Catalina featured the innovative stabilizing floats under the outer wing, which retracted to form aerodynamic wingtips.**

production in 1945, over 4,000 Catalinas had been made, making it the most-produced flying boat in history.

Catalinas were operated by many air arms around the world, including Australia, Brazil, France, the Netherlands, New Zealand, South Africa and the Soviet Union. A number remain in civilian use today and are popular attractions at air shows.

ABOVE: **Early examples of the Catalina were pure flying boats, and the undercarriaged, amphibious version did not appear until 1939. Used by the Allies in all theatres, the Catalina excelled at mine-laying, bombing, air-sea rescue and anti-submarine duties. It was a classic combat aircraft.**

Consolidated PBY-5A Catalina

First flight: March 1935
Power: Two Pratt & Whitney 1,200hp R-1830-92 Twin Wasp 14-cylinder radial engines
Armament: Two 0.5in machine-guns in bow turret and one in each beam blister; one 0.30in machine-gun in ventral tunnel; plus a war load of up to 1,814kg/4,000lb of bombs, mines or depth charges, or two torpedoes
Size: Wingspan – 31.70m/104ft
Length – 19.45m/63ft 10in
Height – 6.15m/20ft 2in
Wing area – 130m²/1,400sq ft
Weights: Empty – 9,485kg/20,910lb
Maximum take-off – 16,067kg/35,420lb
Performance: Maximum speed – 288kph/179mph
Service ceiling – 4,480m/14,700ft
Range – 4,095km/2,545 miles
Climb – 189m/620ft per minute

LEFT AND BELOW:
Consolidated and
Sikorsky were competing
to produce a Catalina
replacement with better
all-round performance
and capability.
Consolidated won with
the XPB2Y-1 (pictured)
but had to revise the tail
with B-24-type fins to
improve stability.

Consolidated PB2Y Coronado

The XPB2Y-1 prototype of what came to be known in British service as the Coronado first flew in December 1937 and within eight months was delivered to the US Navy for service evaluation. Six examples of the first production version, the PB2Y-2, went into service for trials in January 1941. The type was designed to meet a US Navy requirement for a larger and more powerful maritime patrol bomber to replace Consolidated's own PBY Catalina. Although the prototype had flown in 1937, the US Navy did not at that point have the funding to place a major order. Accordingly, it was not until 1941 that the type was ordered in quantity, resulting in the US Navy eventually acquiring 200 examples of the PB2Y-3 – this was an improved PB2Y-2 with self-sealing fuel tanks, more machine-guns and, on later production examples, ASV radar.

This impressive deep-hulled aircraft had a large cantilever wing and twin oval tail fins with a Consolidated family

resemblance to those of the B-24 Liberator. Like the PBY Catalina, the PB2Y featured the innovative floats that retracted to become wingtips thus reducing drag and increasing range.

A number of Coronados, designated PB2Y-3R, were converted for transport duties by having most military equipment removed and turrets faired over. This version could carry 44 passengers and 7,257kg/15,999lb of cargo or 24 stretcher cases and 3,900kg/8,598lb of cargo. The PB2Y-5H, used in the Pacific, was a naval ambulance version of the Coronado that could carry 25 stretchers. US Navy PB2Ys also saw combat in the Pacific, carrying out anti-submarine and bombing missions.

In 1943, another ten examples of the PB2Y-3 were supplied under Lend-Lease

arrangements to the RAF and were designated Coronado I. These aircraft were operated by Coastal and then Transport Command who used them on transatlantic and Caribbean routes.

One PB2Y survives, preserved in the US at Pensacola's National Museum of Naval Aviation.

Consolidated PB2Y-5 Coronado

First flight: December 17, 1937 (prototype)

Power: Four Pratt & Whitney 1,200hp R-1830-92 radial engines

Armament: Six 0.50in machine-guns in three powered turrets, two machine-guns in waist positions, two torpedoes or up to 5,450kg/ 12,000lb of bombs or depth charges housed internally or beneath the wings

Size: Wingspan – 35m/115ft, 24.2m/79ft 3in
Height – 8.4m/27ft 6in
Wing area – 165m²/1,780sq ft

Weights: Empty – 18,530kg/40,850lb
Maximum take-off – 30,000kg/66,139lb

Performance: Maximum speed – 310kph/194mph
Ceiling – 9,181m/30,100ft
Range – 1,720km/1,070 miles
Climb – 174m/570ft per minute

ABOVE: **A PB2Y-3R on take-off. This was a transport conversion by the Rohr Aircraft Co. for Naval Air Transport Service from the PB2Y-3 with the turrets removed and a side hatch added.**

LEFT: **The model that featured a retractable undercarriage was passed over by the US Army but welcomed by the US Navy.**

BELOW: **The Curtiss Hawk family that included the US Navy BFC-2s spanned 15 years of production at a time when aviation technology was gathering real pace.**

Curtiss BFC-2/B2FC-1

The single-seat unequal-span Curtiss Hawk II biplane was part of the large family of aircraft that began with the Curtiss Models 34 and 35 in the mid to late 1920s. Developed from the P-6E, Hawk II demonstrator aircraft flew all over the world and secured a number of overseas orders. The US Navy acquired two examples for testing and decided they had development potential. The USN first ordered 28 examples of the F11C-2 production version powered by a 600hp Wright Cyclone and had them fitted with a bomb 'crutch' for a 227kg/500lb bomb beneath the fuselage – this was to be used for dive-bombing. This version entered USN squadron service with VF-1B aboard USS *Saratoga* in 1933 and was redesignated BFC-2 to reflect its fighter-bomber role. These aircraft, officially though rarely called Goshawks, were in service until 1938.

The US Navy also procured a variant with manually retracted landing gear. This version was designated XF11C-3 by the Navy and Model 67A by the manufacturer. The XF11C-3 was delivered to the US Navy in May 1933. Powered by a 700hp Wright R-1820-80 radial engine, tests found the -3 to be 27.5kph/17mph faster than the -2 though with reduced manoeuvrability due to the weight increase. Speed was the requirement so the type was ordered but changed from the XF11C-3 to the XBF2C-1.

Twenty-seven BF2C-1s were ordered by the US Navy, with a raised rear 'turtledeck' spine, a semi-enclosed cockpit, and a metal-framed lower wing. Armed with two Browning machine-guns and three hardpoints for up to 227kg/500lb of external stores, the aircraft were delivered in October 1934. Assigned to VB-5B aboard USS *Ranger*, the type only served until 1937 having been withdrawn due to incurable problems with undercarriage operation and the aircraft's wing becoming weakened by the accumulated stresses of dive-bombing.

This was a shabby end to the last Curtiss fighter accepted for service with the US Navy. Most were simply ditched in San Diego Bay. Export versions with wooden rather than metal wings

continued to fly in China and Siam for several years, and Chinese machines saw action against the Japanese.

Curtiss BF2C-1

First flight: May 1933 (XF11C-3 prototype)
Power: One Wright 750hp R-1820F-53
Armament: Two 0.30in machine-guns and underwing racks for up to 210kg/464kg of bombs
Size: Wingspan – 9.58m/31ft 6in
Length – 7.16m/23ft 6in
Height – 3.05m/10ft
Wing area – 24.34m²/262sq ft
Weights: Empty – 1,406kg/3,100lb
Maximum take-off – 2,307kg/5,086lb
Performance: Maximum speed – 368kph/228mph
Ceiling – 8,230m/27,000ft
Range – 1,282km/797 miles
Climb – 655m/2,150ft per minute

LEFT: **A Curtiss H-16 of the United States Navy.**

ABOVE: **UK flying boat pioneer Lt John Porte aboard the *America*, which led to the H series and Britain's Felixstowe flying boats. Porte was to have co-piloted the transatlantic aircraft.**

Curtiss H Series Flying Boats

Flying boat pioneer Glenn Curtiss was born in Hammondsport, New York, in 1878. After working as a bicycle mechanic he set up his own motorcycle factory in 1902. Curtiss became interested in aviation and his company began manufacturing airship engines then moved on to building aircraft. In 1908 Curtiss' *June Bug* completed the world's first one-kilometre flight and over the following years he set a series of high-profile records. Curtiss produced the world's first practical seaplane in 1911 then set about designing a flying boat with which he hoped to cross the Atlantic.

Record-breaking flights ceased when World War I broke out, but Curtiss managed to sell two of his H-12 aircraft – derived from the transatlantic flight attempt aircraft – to the Royal Naval Air

Service in Britain. The RNAS were so impressed, they ordered a total of 84 examples before the war's end. A further 20 were ordered for the US Navy – the latter machines were powered by 200hp Curtiss V-2-3 engines. The RNAS considered the H-12s to be underpowered for their size so the aircraft were re-engined first with 275hp Rolls-Royce Eagle Is and later with 375hp Eagle VIIIs, these variants being designated H-12A and H-12B. The US Navy machines were also re-engined but with 360hp Liberty engines and these aircraft were then known as H-12Ls. The US Navy aircraft did not see action in Europe, instead being held to patrol home waters looking for German submarines. The RNAS H-12s, operating from bases in Britain and Ireland, were tasked with anti-Zeppelin patrols and

containing the threat of German U-boats. Capable of flying long ocean patrols and armed with four machine-guns and bombs, the aircraft could easily destroy airships or U-boats. On May 14, 1917, an H-12 shot down a Zeppelin over the North Sea – this was the first ever enemy aircraft to fall to the guns of a US-built aircraft. It was just six days later that an H-12 became the first aircraft to win a victory over a submarine.

The Curtiss H-16 was a development of the H-12 and was built in greater numbers than any other twin-engined Curtiss flying boat. With a hydrodynamically improved hull and more armament, the first H-16 was flown on March 27, 1918. US Navy examples did see service in France, based on the coast to carry out long-range anti-submarine patrols.

LEFT: **The Felixstowe flying boats that were derived from the Curtiss H Series were widely used as patrol aircraft over the North Sea, often fighting enemy aircraft, as well as hunting U-boats and Zeppelins. Later versions served in the Mediterranean. The H Series were an important 'family' of flying boats that saw much action.**

Curtiss H-16

First flight: March 27, 1918
Power: Two 400hp Liberty 12A in-line piston engines
Armament: Six 0.303in machine-guns and up to 417kg/920lb of bombs
Size: Wingspan – 28.97m/95ft 1in
Length – 14.05m/46ft 1.5in
Height – 5.4m/17ft 9in
Wing area – 108.14m²/1164sq ft
Weights: Empty – 3,357kg/7,400lb
Maximum take-off – 4,944g/10,900lb
Performance: Maximum speed – 153kph/95mph
Ceiling – 3,030m/9,950ft
Range – 608km/378 miles
Climb – 3,050m/10,000ft in 29 minutes, 49 seconds

LEFT: **The very unusual means of operation meant that the Sparrowhawks were highly publicized even though only six production aircraft were delivered. One is preserved at the Smithsonian in the US.**

Curtiss F9C-2 Sparrowhawk

First flight: April, 1932 (XF9C-2)

Power: One Wright 438hp R-975-E radial piston engine

Armament: Two fixed fuselage-mounted 0.3in machine-guns

Size: Wingspan – 7.77m/25ft 6in
Length – 6.13m/20ft 1.5in
Height – 3.24m/10ft 7in
Wing area – 16.05m²/173sq ft

Weights: Empty – 948kg/2,089lb
Maximum take-off – 1,261kg/2,779lb

Performance: Maximum speed – 283kph/176mph
Ceiling – 5,850m/19,200ft
Range – 478km/297 miles
Climb – 515m/1,690ft per minute

Curtiss F9C Sparrowhawk

The F9C was designed to meet a 1930 US Navy requirement for a small carrier-borne naval fighter that could operate from existing carriers without the need for folding wings. Curtiss' response was the F9C. This aircraft, along with other contenders, was rejected for carrier operations by the Navy but was deemed suitable to operate from the US Navy's new giant airship, the USS *Akron*. Incredibly, the 240m/785ft-long airship that was

designed for strategic maritime reconnaissance duties had a hangar built inside it, big enough to hold four F9Cs.

The aircraft were launched and recovered by a trapeze that was lowered through large doors which opened in the underside of the *Akron*. Entering service in September 1932, the aircraft had a hook fixed to the top of the fuselage that caught the trapeze, which would then raise the aircraft up into the hangar

without the need to fold the small fighter's wings. The Sparrowhawk retained a standard undercarriage for land operations although experiments saw the removal of the landing gear and replacement with an extra fuel tank. The loss of the *Akron* and her sister ship the *Macon* in 1933 and 1935 put an end to this unique manifestation of naval air power.

LEFT: **Gruelling test-flying showed that the original parasol monoplane configuration was structurally unsuitable for a dive-bombing aircraft so the SBC bucked the trend of the time and the monoplane became a biplane again.**

Curtiss SBC-4 Helldiver

First flight: December 9, 1935 (XSBC-2)

Power: One Wright 900hp Wright R-1820-34 Cyclone 9 radial piston engine

Armament: Two 0.3in machine-guns plus one 227kg/500lb bomb

Size: Wingspan – 10.36m/34ft
Length – 8.57m/28ft 1.5in
Height – 3.17m/10ft 5in
Wing area – 29.45m²/317sq ft

Weights: Empty – 2,065kg/4,552lb
Maximum take-off – 3,211kg/7,080lb

Performance: Maximum speed – 377kph/234mph
Service ceiling – 7,315m/24,000ft
Range – 949km/590 miles
Climb – 567m/1,860ft per minute

Curtiss SBC Helldiver

The Curtiss SBC Helldiver was the last military biplane to enter US Navy service and was an aircraft whose role was changed not once but twice during its development, which saw the design alter from monoplane to biplane. Conceived as a two-seat monoplane fighter (the XF12C-1), it was then designated as a scout and finally as

a scout-bomber. During dive tests for this latter role, the parasol monoplane configuration was found to be structurally weak for dive-bombing so a redesign led to a biplane layout. The eventual production aircraft, the SBC-3, was delivered to the US Navy in July 1937, some four years after the flight testing of the XF12C-1.

The more powerfully engined SBC-4 appeared in 1939 and some of these machines, destined for France before its invasion, were diverted to the RAF who designated them the Cleveland. One USMC and two USN front-line squadrons were still operating the SBC-4 when the US entered World War II but they were withdrawn in early 1942.

LEFT: **The Curtiss SB2C Helldiver was appropriately named according to some of its critics. Structural shortcomings and poor low-speed handling were its main faults, but the type packed a real punch and sank more enemy shipping than any other dive-bomber. It was a very important Allied naval aircraft in World War II.**

Curtiss SB2C Helldiver

The Curtiss SB2C was the third Curtiss aircraft supplied to the US Navy to be called Helldiver but this aircraft shared little in common with the earlier aircraft except its name. The SB2C was developed to replace the Douglas SBD Dauntless and was a much larger aircraft able to operate from the latest aircraft carriers of the time. It carried a considerable array of ordnance and featured an internal bomb bay that reduced drag when carrying heavy weapon loads. The SB2C Helldiver is another aircraft whose contribution to the final Allied victory in World War II is often underestimated.

Manufacturers faced demanding requirements from the USMC and USAAF, and responded by incorporating features of a 'multi-role' aircraft into the design. The first two prototypes crashed, one due to structural failure. This would have sealed the fate of many new aircraft, but as large-scale production had already been ordered in late 1940, a large number of significant modifications were identified for the production model.

Development and production was delayed to the point that Grumman's Avenger, which entered development two years later than the Helldiver, entered service before the Curtiss machine. The many modifications and changes on the production line meant that the Curtiss Helldiver did not enter combat until November 1943 with VB-17 operating from the USS *Bunker Hill*, when they carried out a strike against the Japanese-held port of Rabaul in Papua New Guinea.

Even though the Helldiver was in service, concerns about structural problems meant that crews were forbidden to dive-bomb in 'clean' conditions. This did nothing to endear it to the crews who had relinquished their lighter and smaller SBD Dauntless in favour of what came to be known as 'the beast', partly because of its poor handling at low speeds.

Curtiss Helldiver production at Columbus, Ohio, was supplemented by the output of two Canadian factories. Fairchild Aircraft Ltd (Canada) produced 300 aircraft all

ABOVE: **Some of the prototype's instability issues were resolved by the introduction of an enlarged tail, which led to one of its nicknames – the 'big-tailed beast'. Note the large glazed cockpits.**

ABOVE: **Despite a difficult start, the SB2C made a major contribution to the Allied victory in the Pacific. Its range of over 1,900km/1,200 miles meant it could cover great areas of the Pacific in search of its targets.**

LEFT: The Helldiver was an all-metal, low wing cantilever monoplane. Its wings folded up to save space on carrier decks – note the arrester hook.
BELOW: The trailing edge flaps were perforated to act as dive-brakes and crews were not allowed to dive the aircraft unless it was carrying external ordnance.

designated SBF while Canadian Car and Foundry built 894 examples all designated SBW.

Despite all the problems, the Helldiver became the most successful Allied dive-bomber of World War II and certainly made a major contribution to the successful outcome of the war in the Pacific. The aircraft eventually had good range, making it a very useful weapon for action in the great expanse of the Pacific. The aircraft also packed a significant punch and could carry 454kg/1,000lb of bombs under its wings while a torpedo or another 454kg/1,000lb of ordnance could be carried in the internal bomb bay.

Later improvements to this already more than capable combat aircraft included an uprated Wright Cyclone engine and hardpoints for carrying rocket-projectiles.

The Helldiver saw considerable action in the battles of the Philippine Sea and Leyte Gulf, and played a significant part in the destruction of the Japanese battleships *Yamato* and *Musashi*. As the Allies moved towards the Japanese home islands, Helldivers were active in the Inland Sea and helped deal the deathblow to the Japanese Navy.

Although 26 examples of the SBW-1 version were supplied to the Royal Navy under Lend-Lease, these Fleet Air Arm machines did not see operational service. A total of 450 were

in fact ordered but after FAA testing determined that the aircraft had "appalling handling", the order was cancelled.

Curtiss also built 900 examples of a Helldiver version for the USAAF, designated A-25A Shrike. None saw service with the USAAF and many were converted to SB2C-1 standard for the USMC.

Post-war, Helldivers were the only bombers in the US Navy and continued to equip USN units until 1948 when the Douglas Skyraider was introduced.

Other post-war operators of the Helldiver included the Italian, Greek and Portuguese navies. Helldivers fought on with the French Navy and were used by them in Indochina. Thailand took delivery of six Helldivers in 1951 and retired the aircraft in 1955.

ABOVE: This aircraft is preserved in the US by the Commemorative Air Force and is the last Helldiver still flying. It is an SB2C-5, the last production variant of the aircraft, and served in the US Navy from 1945–48.

Curtiss SB2C-4 Helldiver

First flight: December 18, 1940
Power: One Wright 1,900hp Wright R-2600-20 Cyclone radial engine
Armament: Two 20mm cannon in wings, two 0.3in machine-guns in rear cockpit; 454kg/1,000lb of bombs or a torpedo carried internally plus an additional 454kg/1,000lb of bombs and rocket projectiles carried under wings
Size: Wingspan – 15.16m/49ft 9in
　　　Length – 11.17m/36ft 8in
　　　Height – 4.01m/13ft 2in
　　　Wing area – 39.2m²/422sq ft
Weights: Empty – 4,784kg/10,547lb
　　　　Maximum take-off – 7,537kg/16,616lb
Performance: Maximum speed – 434kph/270mph
　　　　　Service ceiling – 8,870m/29,100ft
　　　　　Range – 1,987km/1,235 miles
　　　　　Climb – 549m/1,800ft per minute

Curtiss SO3C-1 Seamew

The Curtiss SO3C was a two-seat scout monoplane developed in 1937 to replace the US Navy's Curtiss Seagull biplanes. For a time, the SO3C was also, imaginatively, called Seagull. From the outset the aircraft was designed with versatility in mind and could operate from land bases, carrier decks or from water thanks to easily interchangeable float and undercarriage assemblies. The aircraft never lived up to its early promise.

Having beaten competing prototypes for the sizeable contract, the type was found to have major stability problems, which the manufacturers tried to remedy by the addition of upturned wingtips and an enlarged tail surface. While the wingtip modification was a good idea, the enlarged fin was unfortunately not. The base of the enlarged fin extended over, and was in part attached to, the sliding rear cockpit canopy. As the canopy opened and closed, then so did the section of the fin thereby reducing its effectiveness. Most aircraft don't have their canopies open during flight but the SO3C was an observation aircraft and the crewman at the rear of the aircraft often slid his 'greenhouse' canopy forward for a clear view of the sea below. The type first entered service in July 1942 aboard USS *Cleveland*, and crews generally found the SO3C to be difficult and unpleasant to fly.

When the SO3C was chosen for Royal Navy service under Lend-Lease, it was named Seamew, a name which universally replaced the confusing and repetitive Seagull. Although 250 were destined for Fleet Air Arm use, only 100 were in fact accepted and the type never saw operational service. The Seamew (nicknamed 'Seacow' by British crews) entered RN service in January 1944 and was declared obsolete in September

ABOVE: **A pilot runs up the Ranger engine on his SO3C, a very unsatisfactory naval aircraft that saw just 18 months US Navy service. Note the upturned wingtips introduced to improve stability.**

the same year. Relegated to secondary duties, the majority of the British aircraft were used to train FAA crew in Britain and Canada.

Having survived in front-line United States Navy service for only 18 months, the Seamew was replaced by the Seagull biplanes – taken out of mothballs – that it was intended to replace.

Curtiss SO3C-2C (floatplane variant)

First flight: October 6, 1939 (XSO3C-1 prototype)
Power: One Ranger 600hp SVG-770-8 engine
Armament: One 0.3in forward-firing machine-gun, one 0.5in machine-gun on flexible mount in rear crew position plus up to 295kg/650lb of bombs or depth charges carried beneath the wings
Size: Wingspan – 11.58m/38ft
  Length – 11.23m/36ft 10in
  Height – 4.57m/15ft
  Wing area – 26.94m²/290sq ft
Weights: Empty – 1,943kg/4,284lb
  Maximum take-off – 2,599kg/5,729lb
Performance: Maximum speed – 277kph/172mph
  Ceiling – 4,815m/15,800ft
  Range – 1,851km/1,150 miles
  Climb – 220m/720ft per minute

LEFT: **After accepting only 100 examples of the SO3C Seamew, the Royal Navy refused to put the type into front-line service and instead used the Seamews as training aircraft for radio operators and gunners.**

Curtiss F8C-4/02C-1 Helldiver

The aircraft that became the first of three different US Navy Curtiss aircraft called Helldiver was derived from the Curtiss Falcon series. It was designed from the outset as a dive-bomber and had two fixed forward-firing machine-guns fitted to the upper wing. The aircraft's fuselage was made of welded steel tubing while the wings were made of wood.

Although the first prototype crashed in testing, development continued. Among the special features was a bomb rack that launched the Helldiver's 227kg/ 500lb bomb away from the aircraft, as it dived, to avoid the bomb entering the propeller arc.

Like the Curtiss Falcon that inspired it, this aircraft's fuel tanks were 'saddle' tanks, carried on both sides of the aircraft fuselage – how any designer of a fighter aircraft thought that this was ever a good idea defies belief. A single bullet from an enemy aircraft or even small-calibre ground fire could have turned the Helldiver into a fireball.

The first production version was the F8C-4 of which 25 were built. These aircraft served from US Navy carriers from 1930 but were retired from service by the outbreak of World War II.

The US Marine Corps ordered 63 examples of the land-based F8C-5

ABOVE LEFT: **The robust Helldiver was a good aircraft and served the US Navy and Marine Corps for around a decade.** ABOVE: **Favoured for US Navy public relations activity, the type was immortalized on film as being the aircraft used to shoot King Kong as he clung on to the top of New York's Empire State Building.**

variant and a change in the aircraft's primary role from dive-bombing to observation led to their redesignation as the 02C-1. By the time that the US Navy ordered a further 30 examples of the type to operate from carriers, they too were designated 02C-1.

LEFT: **The Helldiver's performance was adequate but not exceptional, and its vulnerable fuel tanks could have cost the US Navy dear in combat. It was some years before self-sealing fuel tanks were developed.**

Curtiss F8C-5/02C-1

First flight: 1928
Power: One Pratt & Whitney 450hp R-1340-4 Wasp radial engine
Armament: Two 0.3in machine-guns and up to 227kg/500lb of bombs or depth charges
Size: Wingspan – 9.75m/32ft
Length – 7.82m/25ft 8in
Height – 3.12m/10ft 3in
Wing area – 28.61m²/308sq ft
Weights: Empty – 1,143kg/2,520lb
Maximum take-off – 1,823kg/4,020lb
Performance: Maximum speed – 235kph/146mph
Ceiling – 4,955m/16,250ft
Range – 1,159km/720 miles
Climb – 289m/948ft per minute

Dornier Do 18

The Dornier Do 18 was designed to replace the military and civil (for Lufthansa) versions of Dornier's Do 15 *Wal* (Whale) flying boat, which had set a number of distance records in its class. The Do 18, first flight March 15, 1935, incorporated a number of innovations and interesting technical features. The flying boat's hull was comprised of seven individual watertight compartments, any two of which could be holed and filled with water without affecting the aircraft's operation. Understanding of aerodynamics and hydrodynamics was growing at the time and the Do 18, though clearly from the same stable, was aerodynamically advanced compared to its Dornier forerunners – its wing tapered, had rounded tips and had the Junkers-style 'double-wing' flap and ailerons.

The Do 18 also had an enclosed cockpit for the side-by-side pilot and co-pilot positions while the radio operator and navigator sat right behind them. A gunner sat in an open compartment between the wing's trailing edge and tail to provide defence against enemy air attack. The aircraft had unique water level sponsons, known as *stümmel*, located directly beneath the wings and joined to them by struts.

ABOVE: **Deutsche Lufthansa received six Do 18s to mainly carry mail across the Atlantic. This aircraft, D-ABYM was named *Aeolus* and was the third example built, hence the designation Do 18 V3.**

Compartmentalized to again minimize the effect of any damage, these stubby wing-like sponsons provided stability in the water and also generated lift in the air. Twin rudders were positioned behind the rear 'step' of the hull to aid steering on the water. Two tandem-mounted diesel engines, one pulling and one pushing atop the wing provided the power, bestowing great range and endurance. The upper rear of the engine housing was beautifully streamlined giving a perfect line to the tip of the propeller spinner. The engines' cooling radiators were housed in a central wing pylon over the aircraft's centreline.

Following its first flight in March 1935, the Do 18 prototype, together with other early examples, joined the Lufthansa fleet operating on South Atlantic services. As an illustration of the Do 18's capabilities, the third prototype, D-ABYM, undertook one test flight in July 1936 that lasted over 30 hours.

ABOVE: **The Do 18G-1 variant introduced a large gun turret on top of the rear fuselage for improved self-defence. Note the large and sturdy *stümmel* beneath the wings, clearly visible as the aircraft is craned.**

ABOVE: **As this Do 18D is preparing to launch, the rear-facing engine of the tandem pair can been seen in action. The D model was the first production series and equipped five front-line units.**

LEFT: A Do 18D of 2./*Kurstenfliegergruppe* 406 about to take off. The lengthy designation means the unit operated in co-operation with the Navy. Note the unit insignia on the starboard side of the forward engine. BELOW: D-ANHR was the Do 18F and was the sixth and the last of the 'mailplanes' delivered to Lufthansa. It first flew on June 11, 1937, and with its larger wing area set a new straight line non-stop distance record for seaplanes in March 1938, covering a distance of 8,392km/5,214 miles.

With three different factories involved in production, the Do 18 entered Luftwaffe service in 1936. By mid-1939, five Luftwaffe front-line units were equipped with Do 18s but by then the type was considered to be obsolete due to its comparatively poor performance and light armament. Nevertheless, it did carry out hazardous reconnaissance duties over the North Sea. On September 26, 1939, a Do 18 became the first German aircraft of World War II to be shot down by British aircraft when a formation of three Do 18s was caught over the North Sea by Royal Navy Blackburn Skuas flying from HMS *Ark Royal* – the victorious pilot was Lieutenant B.S. McEwan.

The Bv 138 was ordered as the Dornier boat's replacement in Luftwaffe service but due to problems with the Blohm und Voss aircraft, an improved version of the Do 18 was hurriedly developed as a stop-gap. The Do 18G-1 had the more powerful 880hp Jumo 205D engine and take-off could also be helped by the use of booster rockets. This version was also better able to defend itself with the addition of a 13mm machine-gun in the open bow position while a 20mm cannon was housed in a power-operated turret that replaced the open gun position over the rear step of the hull.

Production stopped in mid-1940, while the G-1 models replaced the D models still in Luftwaffe service, many of the later variants being shifted to air-sea rescue duties. The Do 18G-1 was gradually withdrawn from service with the last Norway-based machines known to have been withdrawn in the summer of 1941.

ABOVE: This early production Do 18 shows the open bow position and the surface area of the *stümmel* which, as effectively short wings, gave the boat added lift. Note the streamlined engines.

Dornier Do 18G-1

First flight: March 15, 1935 (prototype)
Power: Two Junkers 880hp Jumo 205D diesel piston engines
Armament: One 13mm machine-gun in nose position, one 20mm machine-gun in dorsal turret and up to 100kg/220lb of bombs carried beneath wings
Size: Wingspan – 23.7m/77ft 9in
Length – 19.38m/63ft 7in
Height – 5.32m/17ft 6in
Wing area – 98m²/1,055sq ft
Weights: Empty – 5,978kg/13,180lb
Maximum take-off – 10,795kg/23,800lb
Performance: Maximum speed – 267kph/166mph
Ceiling – 4,200m/13,800ft
Range – 3,500km/2,175 miles
Climb – 1,000m/3,280ft in 7 minutes, 48 seconds

Dornier Do 24

The Do 24 flying boat was produced by Dornier before and during World War II. Originally designed to meet a mid-1930s Dutch Navy requirement for use in the Dutch East Indies (today's Indonesia), the Do 24 was a side-by-side three-engined flying boat intended for military cargo transport and air-sea rescue. Intended to operate far from a home base, the Do 24 had living and sleeping quarters for its then crew of six. Dornier company records claim that up to 12,000 people were rescued by the type in a career that continued through to 1970.

The Dutch specified that, to ease maintenance through compatiblity with other aircraft they operated, the Do 24 was to be engined by Wright Cyclone radials. The prototype flew on July 3, 1937, sea trials followed and the Do 24 soon went into production. Twelve Do 24K-1s were built for the Dutch Navy and then the Dutch began to licence-assemble a further 48 machines that were designated Do 24K-2.

Thirty-seven Dutch and German-built Do 24s had been deployed to the East Indies by the time of the German invasion of Holland in June 1940. Of these machines, six surviving

TOP: **This Do 24N-1 was a Do 24K built in the Netherlands and then modified for service with the Luftwaffe. For a large aircraft it presents surprisingly little frontal area.** ABOVE: **Three prototype Do 24s were built and this aircraft was the Do 24 V3 D-ADLR that was the first to fly on July 3, 1937. Power came from three 890hp Wright Cyclones and the aircraft was delivered to the Dutch for evaluation in late 1937. In Dutch service it was registered as X-1.**

aircraft were transferred to the Royal Australian Air Force in February, 1942, when the Japanese overran their bases. The Do 24s served in the RAAF as transports in New Guinea thereby becoming one of the few aircraft types to serve with both Axis and Allied air arms during World War II.

When the Dutch assembly line was captured by the Germans, the Luftwaffe, hitherto disinterested in the Do 24, pressed for production to continue. Eleven aircraft were completed with Wright Cyclone engines already acquired by the Dutch under the designation Do 24N-1 but subsequent machines were built with German BMW Bramo 323 R-2 radials and were designated Do 24T-1.

A further Do 24 production line was established in France during the German occupation. Operated by SNCA, another 48 Do 24s were built there. The factory was abandoned as the Allied liberation forces swept through France but production resumed soon after making a further 40 Do 24s that served in

ABOVE: **The Do 24T-2 differed from earlier versions by having a 20mm cannon in the dorsal turret seen here just forward of the cross on the fuselage side.**

LEFT: **The 5W on the side of this aircraft tells us it was operated by *Seenotstaffel* 10, an air-sea rescue unit. When not performing the ASR role, these large aircraft were used to move troops and resupply ground troops.** ABOVE: **The 600hp Jumo-powered Do 24 V1 prototype did not fly until 1938, and later saw military service as a transport during the 1940 invasion of Norway.**

the French Air Force until 1952. A German Do 24 that made a forced landing in neutral Sweden during the war was impounded, then paid for, repaired and remained airworthy in Swedish service until 1952.

The Dornier flying boat served with the Luftwaffe on every front of World War II and was equally adept at troop carrying and air-sea rescue. The type also escorted convoys and carried out maritime reconnaissance and could ship great quantities of supplies. Essential resupply missions during the German defence of the Kuban bridgehead in the Caucasus in 1943 saw 22 of these flying boats deliver 1,000 tons – since airstrips in the region were flooded, the Do 24s were the only lifeline available.

The aircraft's ability to operate in the most hostile of conditions earned it a place in aviation history as one of the greatest ocean-going flying boats. The Do 24 rescued airmen and sailors in the Arctic, the Mediterranean, the North Sea,

the English Channel and the Atlantic. One crew was rescued from the Atlantic 563km/350 miles from the nearest land. The best example of the type's ruggedness is the story of the aircraft that lost its tail on landing but taxied back to shore with crew and rescued survivors safe within the watertight remains of the aircraft.

In June 1944, 12 Dutch-built Do 24s were supplied to Spain apparently on the basis that they would rescue downed airmen of both sides. These Spanish machines were augmented post-war by some French-built examples and some remained in service until 1970.

In February 2004, a restored and re-engined example designated Do-24 ATT, began flying around the world to benefit the UNICEF organization. This sole flying example is now operated as a charter aircraft by South East Asian Airlines.

Between 1937 and 1945 the various factories produced a total of 279 Do 24s.

ABOVE: **The sole flying example, the fully restored Do 24 ATT powered by three Pratt & Whitney Canada PT6A-45 turboprop engines. It is now available for charter and gives the lucky passengers a rare experience of taking off from water in a classic flying boat.**

Dornier Do 24T-1

First flight: July 3, 1937 (prototype)
Power: Three 1,000hp BMW-Bramo 323R-2 9-cylinder radial engines
Armament: One 7.9mm machine-gun in bow and stern turrets and one 20mm cannon in dorsal turret
Size: Wingspan – 27m²/88ft 7in
    Length – 22.05m/72ft 4in
    Height – 5.75m/18ft 10in
    Wing area – 108m²/1,163sq ft
Weights: Empty – 9,400kg/20,723lb
    Maximum take-off – 18,400kg/40,565lb
Performance: Maximum speed – 331kph/206mph
    Ceiling – 7,500m/24,605ft
    Range – 4,700km/2,920 miles
    Climb – 2,000m/6,560ft in 6 minutes

Douglas SBD-5 Dauntless

The Douglas SBD Dauntless dive-bomber, a mainstay of the US Navy's World War II air assets in the Pacific, had the lowest loss ratio of any US carrier-based aircraft. The first enemy ship sunk by the US Navy during World War II is credited to a Dauntless from the USS *Enterprise*. The Dauntless went on to destroy 18 enemy warships, including a battleship and six carriers.

The Dauntless had its origins in a 1934 Northrop proposal for a new US Navy dive-bomber, the BT-1, based on the Northrop A-17 light attack bomber. The Northrop machine was the inspiration for Douglas' own XBT-1 which first flew in July 1935. After a series of service trials, an order was placed for 54 BT-1s – the first production examples were fitted with 825hp Wright R-1535-94 engines while the last ones off the production line were fitted with 1,000hp R-11820-32 engines and designated XBT-2. More modifications followed and when the Northrop Corporation became a division of Douglas in August 1937, the aircraft was redesignated XSBD-1.

ABOVE: **Unusually for the time, the Dauntless served with the US Navy, Marines Corps and the USAAF, in the latter case as the A-24. The USAAF machines did not have the arrester hook for carrier operations.**

ABOVE: **Despite its shortcomings, the Dauntless went on to sink more enemy shipping than any other Allied aircraft in the Pacific War. It was the aircraft that won the Battle of Midway and changed the course of the war.**

When prototype testing had proved the design to be outstanding in its field, in April 1939 the US Marine Corps and US Navy placed orders for the SBD-1 and SBD-2 respectively. The Navy machine had increased fuel capacity and different armament. Production commenced in 1940, and although the SBD bore a resemblance to its Northrop predecessor, it was a completely different aircraft. The SBD-1 first entered service with the US Marines in mid-1940 when they received a batch of 57 SBD-1s with their distinctive perforated 'Swiss cheese' flaps – dive brakes punched with 7.62mm/0.3in holes so the aircraft could achieve pinpoint accuracy by diving to the target, dropping the bomb and then pulling out of the near-vertical dive.

The US Navy received its first SBD-2s in early 1941, and by the summer of that year had taken delivery of over 400 SBD-3s – this version had self-sealing, larger fuel tanks as well as armour protection, a bullet-proof windscreen and four machine-guns. By the end of 1941, the Dauntless constituted the attack element of the US Navy's carrier-based air group in the Pacific. In 1941, the US Army, aware that it did not have a dive-bomber in the same class as the Luftwaffe's Ju 87 Stuka, ordered the SBD-3 under the designation A-24. This land-based version was identical to the Navy machines but lacked an arrester hook and sported a tailwheel with an inflatable tyre instead of the solid rubber one used on Navy machines. Although it never lived up to its early promise during World War II, the type remained in US Army Air Corps and then US Air Force use for several years after the war.

The SBD-4 featured an improved 24-volt electrical system and some of these machines became SBD-4P reconnaissance aircraft. It was, however, the SBD-5, built at Douglas's new plant in Tulsa, Oklahoma, that was the most widely produced variant. Powered by a 1,200hp R-1820-60 engine, this version could also carry more ammunition for its guns. Over 2,400 SBD-5s were built – some were supplied to, but never used in action by, the Royal Navy's Fleet Air Arm where they were designated Dauntless DB Mk I. Interestingly, Mexico was the other export customer for the SBD-5. The ultimate version was the SBD-6, with an even more powerful engine and greater fuel capacity.

Douglas delivered a total of 5,936 SBDs and Army Air Forces A-24s between 1940 and the end of production in July 1944. In addition to the US Navy, Marine Corps and Army Air Forces, Britain and Mexico, the Dauntless also served with the Royal New Zealand Navy. Free French machines were used against German forces in France post-D-Day.

TOP: **The two-man crew of the Dauntless sat under a continuous 'greenhouse' canopy with a bullet-proof windscreen. The defensive guns in the rear cockpit were effective and one US Navy Dauntless crew is known to have destroyed seven Japanese Zeros in just two days.** ABOVE: **Note the distinctive perforated 'Swiss cheese' flaps visible as this US Navy machine prepares for take-off.**

Douglas SBD-5 Dauntless

First flight: July 1935

Power: One Wright 1,200hp R-1820-60 Cyclone 9-cylinder radial engine

Armament: Two 0.50in fixed forward-firing machine-guns in the upper part of the forward fuselage; two trainable 0.30in machine-guns in rear cockpit; external bomb or depth-charge load of 1,021kg/2,250lb

Size: Wingspan – 12.66m/41ft 6in
Length – 10.09m/33ft 1in
Height – 4.14m/13ft 7in
Wing area – 30.19m²/325sq ft

Weights: Empty – 2,963kg/6,534lb
Maximum take-off – 4,853kg/10,700lb

Performance: Maximum speed – 410kph/255mph
Service ceiling – 7,780m/25,530ft
Range – 2,519km/1,565 miles
Climb – 457m/1,500ft per minute

ABOVE: **Dauntless pilots would typically approach their target at a maximum altitude of 6,100m/20,000ft. When over their objective, they would deploy both upper and lower dive flaps before diving on the target. A telescopic sight, and later a reflector sight, kept them on target.**

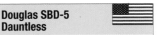

FAR LEFT: **An SBD Dauntless and five Devastators prepare to take off from the *Enterprise* during operations in the South Pacific on May 4, 1942.**

LEFT: **A Devastator, 6-T-19 of Torpedo Squadron Six from the USS *Enterprise* (CV-6), releases its torpedo during exercises in the Pacific, October 20, 1941. There were, however, serious performance deficiencies with the Mk XIII torpedo, which often failed to explode or ran too deep beneath targets. Crews would run the gauntlet of enemy anti-aircraft fire to see the weapon failing. It took a year to perfect the weapon. The aircraft's other main weapon was a single 454kg/1,000lb bomb which would prove devastating when scoring a direct hit on a ship.**

Douglas TBD-1 Devastator

The Douglas TBD-1 was the US Navy's first widely used carrier-borne monoplane. The XTBD-1 prototype first flew on April 15, 1935, and was handed over to the US Navy for testing just nine days later.

This large aircraft, with a wingspan of 15.24m/50ft, was designed to carry a heavy torpedo beneath its fuselage. A total of 129 production TBD-1s were delivered to the USN between 1937 and 1939 replacing biplanes in torpedo squadrons on board US carriers *Saratoga*, *Enterprise*, *Lexington*, *Wasp*, *Hornet*, *Yorktown* and *Ranger*.

With a top speed of around 322kph/200mph, the aircraft was fast in its class for the time. The TBD-1 was the first all-metal aircraft in the US Navy, the first with a fully enclosed cockpit and the first with hydraulically folding wings for carrier operations. With its wings unfolded, the aircraft would take up a lot of room in a cramped carrier hangar so Douglas designed them to fold upwards reducing the span to just 7.92m/26ft. It had a semi-retractable undercarriage and the wheels were designed to protrude 25cm/10in below the wings in the 'up' position to minimize the damage of a wheels-up landing.

A TBD had a crew of three who sat in tandem (pilot, bombardier and gunner/radio operator from front to back) beneath a large greenhouse canopy that ran almost half the length of the aircraft's sleek and curvaceous fuselage. During a bombing run, the bombardier would lay prone having crawled into position beneath the pilot, then aim his weapons (a Mk XIII torpedo or one 454kg/1,000lb bomb) using a Norden bombsight through a window in the bottom of the fuselage.

LEFT: **The TBD's mechanically folded wings was one innovation that made the Devastator possibly the most advanced carrier aircraft in the world for a time. The fast pace of aircraft development, accelerated by the arms race and political tensions of the time, meant this status was shortlived. By the time of the Japanese attack on Pearl Harbor, the TBD was already outdated. The type did, however, fly on until 1943, albeit in training roles.**

The Devastator's defensive armament consisted of one forward-firing 0.30in or 0.5in machine-gun operated by the pilot. The armament can be identified by the presence of a breech fairing blister rear of the starboard air intake – only the Colt/Browning 0.50 calibre M2 required the fairing to be added. The rear gunner also had a 0.30in or a 0.5in machine-gun at this disposal but on a flexible mount.

Around 100 TBD-1s were in service when war broke out, representing the US Pacific Fleet's sole torpedo aircraft for the early stages of the war against Japan. The type served well as a torpedo-bomber and high-level bomber for the first half of 1942 and, on May 7, TBDs were instrumental in the sinking of the Japanese carrier *Shoho* in the Battle of the Coral Sea.

But then the TBD-1 guaranteed its place in history for the worst possible reasons. On June 4, 1942, during the Battle of Midway, three squadrons of TBD-1s made daring but unsuccessful daylight torpedo attacks on the Japanese Imperial Fleet north of Midway Island and lost all but four of the 41 aircraft that began the mission. By then old and slow for the fast-paced air combat environment of the Pacific, with relatively poor defensive armament and no self-sealing fuel tanks, the Devastator was itself devastated by Japanese fighters and anti-aircraft fire. In fairness to the TBD, this was a fate that befell many torpedo-bombers of the time due to the extremely hazardous nature of their mission. Within three years, the TBD-1 had gone from cutting edge to out of date, such was the pace of combat aircraft design performance and tactics.

With the Battle of Midway over, the US Navy had just 39 TBDs left in its front-line inventory and these were rapidly replaced by Grumman Avengers. The surviving TBDs flew on in training units until 1943, or as communication aircraft, and some were used as static instructional airframes through 1944. No TBDs are preserved although an example that ditched in the sea may be recovered for a US museum. Total production was 130 including a floatplane trials aircraft.

ABOVE AND BELOW: **Two 1938 studies of the same aircraft, a TBD-1 from Torpedo Squadron Six (VT-6) operating from USS *Enterprise* (CV-6). The aircraft (Bureau of Aeronautics number 0322) was that of the Torpedo Squadron Six commanding officer and was lost in an accident at sea on March 10, 1939. VT-6 was one of the units mauled during the Battle of Midway due to the lack of co-ordination of fighter escort, as well as attack by numerous enemy fighters.**

ABOVE: **TBD-1 Devastators and Grumman F4F-3 Wildcats parked on the incredibly congested flight deck of the USS *Enterprise*, April 1942. Note the variations in the size of the national insignia on the fuselage sides.**

Douglas TBD-1 Devastator

First flight: April 15, 1935
Power: Pratt & Whitney 900hp R-1830-64 Double Wasp air-cooled radial engine
Armament: Two 0.30in or 0.5in machine-guns plus a Mk XIII torpedo (544kg/1,200lb) or a 454kg/1,000lb bomb
Size: Wingspan – 15.24m/50ft
    Length – 10.69m/35ft
    Height – 4.59m/15ft 1in
    Wing area – 39.2m²/422sq ft
Weights: Empty – 2,804kg/6,182lb
    Maximum take-off – 4,623kg/10,194lb
Performance: Maximum speed – 331kph/206mph
    Ceiling – 6,004m/19,700ft
    Range – 700km/435 miles
    Climb – 222m/720ft per minute

LEFT: **A Fairey IIIB floatplane about to take off. The remarkable longevity of the Fairey III says much about the excellence of the basic design. The IIIB had a larger wing area than the IIIA and was used for mine-spotting from coastal bases.**
ABOVE: **An improved Fairey IIIF Mk IIIB taxis towards a Royal Navy ship.**

Fairey III family

Originally, a World War I twin-float seaplane, the N.10, Fairey converted this general-purpose biplane aircraft into a landplane, the Fairey IIIA, which became one of the company's most successful designs.

This entered Royal Navy service as a two-seat carrier-borne bomber. The IIIB was a floatplane version while the IIIC had a much more powerful engine. The Fairey IIID was the second most numerous variant produced and appeared in RAF landplane but mainly Royal Navy floatplane versions. In the spring of 1926, four RAF Fairey IIIDs carried out a 22,366km/13,900 miles long-distance formation flight from Northolt,

near London, to Cape Town and back through Greece, Italy and France. IIIDs were exported to Australia, Ireland, Chile, Portugal, Sweden and the Netherlands.

The Fairey IIIF, a much-improved development of the IIID was the most numerous variant with 597 aircraft produced. This aircraft, again in landplane and floatplane versions, gave sterling service in the RAF and Fleet Air Arm in Britain and overseas from 1927 until the mid-1930s. The obvious successor to the excellent IIIF was another IIIF, which is what the RAF's Fairey Gordon and Royal Navy Seals were. The two-man Gordon was a IIIF fitted with a different engine and other

minor changes while the Seal was a three-seat naval version with a float conversion option and an arrester hook. Members of this family of aircraft served from World War I through to the early days of World War II – quite an achievement considering the type was thought to be obsolete in 1918.

One complete Fairey III survives, a Mk 2 version of the Fairey III D preserved in the *Museu da Marinha* (Navy Museum) in Portugal. This historic aircraft was involved in a transatlantic crossing attempt by Portugal in 1922.

Fairey III family

First flight: March 19, 1926
Power: One Napier 570hp Lion XIA 12-cylinder V-type engine
Armament: One 0.303in Vickers machine-gun in front fuselage and one 0.303in Lewis gun in rear cockpit, provision for 227kg/500lb bomb load under lower wing
Size: Wingspan – 13.94m/45ft 9in
Length – 11.19m/36ft 8.6in
Height – 4.26m/14ft
Wing area – 40.74m²/439sq ft
Weights: Empty – 1,762kg/3,880lb
Maximum take-off – 2,740kg/6,041lb
Performance: Maximum speed – 193kph/120mph
Service ceiling – 6,700m/22,000ft
Range – 644km/400 miles
Climb – 305m/1,000ft per minute

ABOVE: **A Fairey IIIF Mk IIIB being craned aboard a Royal Navy ship. The service use of this remarkable family of aircraft spanned two World Wars, a rare service record for any aircraft.**

LEFT: **Demonstrating just how much space can be saved by wing-folding, this Albacore has it engine run up while deck crew work on the aircraft.** ABOVE: **The Albacore introduced many 'luxuries' for the three-man crew including an enclosed, heated cabin but it was outlasted by the aircraft it was intended to replace in FAA service.** BELOW: **From mid-1942, the Fleet Air Arm was operating large numbers of the Fairey biplane from the Mediterranean to the Arctic Circle. In all, 800 aircraft were built but the type was retired from the FAA by the end of 1943.**

Fairey Albacore

Designed in response to a British Air Ministry specification S.41/36 for a torpedo/reconnaissance bomber to replace the Swordfish, the single-engine three-seat Albacore was expected to be a great improvement over the earlier Fairey aircraft. Despite having an all-metal fuselage and having features including an enclosed, heated cockpit and automatic emergency dinghy ejection, the Albacore was in fact outlasted in service by the venerable Swordfish. Although more streamlined than the Swordfish and able to reach greater altitudes, the Albacore had lower cruising speed and a shorter range than the older aircraft. To add insult to injury, the Albacore was also used to train Swordfish crews and Swordfish production continued for a year after the Albacore was removed from front-line duties.

The first prototype had its maiden flight in December 1938, the type having been ordered into production from plans 18 months earlier. Production began in 1939 and on March 15, 1940, No.826 Squadron at Ford became the first unit to receive the type. The squadron was in action on May 31 carrying out attacks against E-boats off the Dutch coast as well as inland targets in Belgium. By the end of 1940 there were a further

three UK land-based units operating the type carrying out duties from anti-submarine patrols and mine-laying to shipping strikes. Two of the Albacore squadrons, Nos.826 and 829, embarked on HMS *Formidable* in November 1940, and in March 1941 took part in the type's first torpedo strikes in attacks on the Italian battleship *Vittorio Veneto* during the Battle of Cape Matapan.

Fifteen Fleet Air Arm squadrons were equipped with the Albacore by mid-1942 and the type went on to see action in the Arctic, Western Desert, Indian Ocean and the Mediterranean as well as in UK home waters and the Channel. During the Allied invasion of North Africa, Albacores carried out coastal gun suppression and anti-submarine missions. During and immediately after the Allied invasion of Normandy, Albacores operated by the Royal Canadian Air Force were tasked with the suppression of German E-boats attempting to interfere with Allied shipping.

The Albacore was retired before the Swordfish, and from 1942 was gradually replaced by the Fairey Barracuda and

Grumman Avenger. One Albacore survives, preserved by the Fleet Air Arm Museum at Yeovilton in the UK.

Fairey Albacore	

First flight: December 12, 1938

Power: One Bristol 1,130hp Taurus XII radial engine

Armament: One forward-firing 0.303in machine-gun in starboard wing, two 0.303in machine-guns in rear cockpit plus one 730kg/1,610lb torpedo hung under fuselage or four 227kg/500lb bombs beneath the wings

Size: Wingspan – 15.24m/50ft
    Length – 12.14m/39ft 10in
    Height – 4.32m/14ft 2in
    Wing area – 57.88m²/623sq ft

Weights: Empty – 3,289kg/7,250lb
    Maximum take-off – 4,745kg/10,460lb

Performance: Maximum speed – 259kph/161mph
    Ceiling – 6,310m/20,700ft
    Range – 1,497km/930 miles
    Climb – 1,829m/6,000ft in 8 minutes

Fairey Barracuda

Fairey's response to the Royal Navy-led specification S.24/37 for a Fairey Albacore replacement was the three-seat Barracuda which had its maiden flight on December 7, 1940. Testing highlighted some shortcomings that were resolved in the second prototype but this did not fly until June 1941 – Britain's aviation industry was focusing on the production of fighters and bombers at the time and the new torpedo-bomber just had to wait. Service trials were consequently not completed until February 1942 after which the more powerful Merlin 32 was fitted. The new engine was required to cope with the increasing weight of the Barracuda due to a beefing-up of the structure and additional equipment that had to be carried. The re-engined Barracuda became the Mk II and was the main production variant of the type. The Mk IIs began to enter service in early 1943, the first Mk IIs

ABOVE: The design that became Fairey's Barracuda beat off five other proposals that all responded to the request for an Albacore successor. Note the deployed Fairey-Youngman trailing edge flaps that aided the type's all-round performance. BELOW LEFT: Looking bug-like with its folded wings, the Barracuda served the Royal Navy in quantity although not all pilots liked the aircraft. Forty-two of these pugnacious aircraft attacked the *Tirpitz* in April 1944.

going to No.827 Squadron then re-forming at Stretton. By May 1943, many squadrons of the Fleet Air Arm became fully equipped with Barracuda Mk IIs and then joined carriers of the Home and Far Eastern fleets.

The Barracuda had a number of claims to fame – it was the first British carrier-based monoplane of all-metal construction to enter service with the Fleet Air Arm as well as being the first monoplane torpedo-bomber. A total of 1,688 Barracuda Mk IIs were built by Fairey as well as Westland, Blackburn and Boulton Paul.

The Barracuda Mk III (912 examples built by Fairey and Boulton Paul) was developed to carry ASV (air-to-surface vessel) radar in a radome blister under the rear fuselage, and first flew in 1943. The radar enabled the Barracuda to track its prey much more effectively. In European waters, Mk IIIs equipped with ASV radar flew anti-submarine patrols from small escort carriers using Rocket-Assisted Take-Off (RATO) to get clear of the short decks.

In April 1944, the carriers *Victorious* and *Furious* sent 42 Barracudas to carry out a dive-bombing attack on the German pocket battleship *Tirpitz* then at anchor in Kaa Fjord, Norway. The Barracudas were part of Operation 'Tungsten', the aim of which was the destruction of the enemy battleship. The Barracudas had practised long and hard for the operation and attacked in a steep dive despite heavy defensive flak. They scored 15 direct hits with armour-piercing bombs for the loss

of only two aircraft. *Tirpitz* was so damaged in the raid that it was out of action for three months and the Navy was able to channel its resources elsewhere, at least for a time.

Nos.810 and 847 Squadrons, Fleet Air Arm, embarked on HMS *Illustrious*, introduced the Barracuda to the Pacific theatre of operations in April 1944 when they supported the US Navy in a dive-bombing attack on the Japanese installations on Sumatra.

In all, 23 operational Fleet Air Arm squadrons were equipped with Barracudas during World War II. Wartime production of the Fairey Barracuda totalled 2,541 aircraft. In 1945 production started on the more powerful Mk V, later designated the TF.5, but only 30 models of this variant were built and were used as trainers during the post-war period.

A total of 2,572 Barracudas of all marks were delivered to the Fleet Air Arm. Barracudas were also operated by the French and Dutch Fleet Air Arms.

ABOVE: **Despite its ungainly appearance, the Barracuda could carry out a wide variety of missions well. The high-winged Fairey aircraft was progressively and successfully modified to carry bombs, mines, torpedoes, depth charges, rockets, radar masts and radomes, lifeboats and even containers under the wings for dropping agents into occupied territory.**

Fairey Barracuda Mk II

First flight: December 7, 1940
Power: One Rolls-Royce 1640hp Merlin 32 V-12 piston engine
Armament: Two 0.303in Browning machine-guns in rear cockpit; one 735kg/1,620lb torpedo or one 454kg/1,000lb bomb beneath fuselage, or four 204kg/450lb or six 113kg/250lb bombs, depth charges or mines under wings
Size: Wingspan – 14.99m/49ft 2in
    Length – 12.12m/39ft 9in
    Height – 4.60m/15ft 1in
    Wing area – 34.09m²/367sq ft
Weights: Empty – 4,241kg/9,350lb
    Maximum take-off – 6,396kg/14,100lb
Performance: Maximum speed – 367kph/228mph
    Service ceiling – 5,060m/16,600ft
    Range – 1,851km/1,150 miles
    Climb – 1,524m/5,000ft in 6 minutes

Fairey Firefly

From 1926, Britain's Fleet Air Arm deployed a series of fast two-seat multi-role fighter reconnaissance aircraft. The Fairey Firefly, designed by H.E. Chaplin at Fairey Aviation in 1940, continued the tradition having been designed to meet Admiralty specification N.5/40. Even before it had flown the design showed enough promise that, in June 1940, the Admiralty ordered 200 aircraft.

The prototype Firefly flew on December 22, 1941, and although it was 2 tons heavier than the Fulmar it was to replace (due mainly to its armament of two 20mm cannon in the wings), the Firefly was 64kph/40mph faster due to a better understanding of aerodynamics and a more powerful engine, the 1,730hp Rolls-Royce Griffon. It was, however, still slower than most contemporary fighters but possessed great low-speed handling characteristics that are vital for a carrier-borne fighter.

TOP: **This Firefly AS.5 served with both the Royal Navy and Royal Australian Navy. It was restored and kept in flying condition but was lost in a fatal crash in 2003.** ABOVE: **The early Firefly production versions had the radiator intake below the engine as can be seen on this aircraft. Notice the four cannon protruding from the wing leading edges.**

ABOVE: **In all versions, including this anti-submarine mark, the observer's position was behind the wing while the pilot sat over the leading edge. The Firefly served in the front-line ASW role until the mid-1950s.**

The main variant in use during World War II was the F. Mk I, which saw action in all theatres of operations following first deliveries in March 1943 although they did not enter operational service until July 1944 equipping No.1770 Squadron on board HMS *Indefatigable*. The type's first operations were in Europe where Fireflies made armed reconnaissance flights and anti-shipping strikes along the Norwegian coast. Fireflies also provided air cover during the July 1944 sinking of the German battleship *Tirpitz* lying at anchor in Kaa Fjord, Northern Norway.

Firefly night-fighter variants were developed early in production of the type and carried airborne interception radar in small wing-mounted radomes. The associated extra equipment affected the aircraft's centre of gravity and necessitated a lengthening of the fuselage by 45.7cm/18in. This version of the F.1, the N.F.2, was only produced in limited quantities because an alternative means of accommodating the radar equipment was developed that did not require major structural work. Radar was then being fitted as standard to Fireflies and the non-lengthened Firefly N.F.1 was the night-fighter version of the F.R.1 which was itself basically an F.1 fitted with radar. All Firefly night-fighters were equipped with exhaust dampers so that the glowing exhausts of the Griffin would not show up in darkness. During late 1944, Fireflies operated by the Night Fighter Interception Unit based at RAF Coltishall in Norfolk undertook night patrols to counter V1 flying bombs air-launched over the North Sea by Luftwaffe He 111s.

Although the Firefly was never a classic fighter, it excelled in the strike and armed reconnaissance role. Despite this, the first Firefly air combat victory occurred on January 2, 1945, during a Fleet Air Arm attack on oil refineries in Sumatra when a No.1770 Squadron aircraft shot down a Japanese Nakajima Ki-43 'Oscar', a very capable dogfighter.

Throughout its operational career, the Firefly took on increasingly more demanding roles, from fighter to anti-submarine warfare. It was stationed mainly with the British Pacific Fleet in the Far East and Pacific theatres. In January 1945, the first major action by the Fleet Air Arm against the Japanese saw oil refineries in Sumatra set ablaze by rockets fired from Fireflies.

Fireflies entered the history books when they became the first British-designed and built aircraft to overfly Tokyo at the end of World War II. In the weeks immediately after VJ day, Fleet Air Arm Fireflies carried out supply drops to POW camps on the Japanese mainland.

Post-war the Firefly remained in service in the UK, Canada and Australia. The Royal Canadian Navy deployed 65 Fireflies of the Mk AS.5 type on board its carriers between 1946 and 1954. Fleet Air Arm Fireflies carried out anti-shipping missions from aircraft carriers in the Korean War (as did Australian Fireflies) as well as serving in the ground-attack role in Malaya. In 1956, the Firefly's FAA front-line career ended with the introduction of the Fairey Gannet in the ASW role.

ABOVE: **Many types developed in World War II were in action again in Korea including Royal Navy Seafires, Sea Furies and Fireflies (pictured). The Royal Navy only operated propeller aircraft in the war.**

ABOVE: **An ASW Firefly catches the wire. Notice the wing leading-edge radiators that typified the later versions, and the black and white 'D-Day' type stripes applied to all FAA aircraft that fought in Korea.**

ABOVE: **The Firefly was built at two Fairey factories at Hayes in Middlesex and Heaton Chapel on the outskirts of Manchester. General Aircraft were also subcontracted to build the type.**

Fairey Firefly F.1

First flight: December 22, 1941
Power: Rolls-Royce 1,990hp Griffon XII
Armament: Four 20mm cannon in wings
Size: Wingspan – 13.56m/44ft 6in
(4.04m/13ft 3in folded)
Length – 11.46m/37ft 7in
Height – 4.14m/13ft 7in
Wing area – 30.48m²/328sq ft
Weights: Empty – 4,423kg/9,750lb
Maximum take-off weight – 6,360kg/14,020lb
Performance: Maximum speed –
509kph/316mph
Ceiling – 8,534m/28,000ft
Range – 2,092km/1,300 miles
Climb – 4,575m/15,000ft in 9 minutes,
36 seconds

Fairey Flycatcher

The Flycatcher was conceived to meet a 1922 British Air Ministry specification that called for a new versatile single-seat Royal Navy carrier-based fighter that could be configured as a floatplane or amphibian. Power was to be provided by either the Armstrong Siddeley Jaguar or the Bristol Jupiter radial engines. The Flycatcher first flew on November 28, 1922, powered by a Jaguar III engine. After competitive service evaluation trials the Flycatcher was ordered for full production.

The Flycatcher with its fabric-covered mixed wood/metal fuselage was a remarkable aircraft for 1922 as it was one of the first aircraft specifically designed to operate from aircraft

carriers. Full length flaps on the wings bestowed great lift so the aircraft only needed 45.75m/150ft in which to land or take off without the need for arrester wires or a catapult. The Flycatcher was also designed to 'break down' easily into sections no longer than 4.11m/13ft 6in for transportation, and the aircraft was already small enough to fit on the aircraft carrier lifts of the time without folding its wings. The undercarriage could be changed for twin floats or even a wheel/float combination for amphibian operations. It was a staggered-wing biplane of unequal span and had a tail skid instead of a tailwheel.

The Flycatcher first entered service with No.402 Flight Fleet Air Arm in 1923 and went on to be flown from all the

ABOVE: **The Fairey Flycatcher was a delight to fly, although it was not a high-performance aircraft. It was, however, versatile.**

British carriers of its era. Some aircraft operated as turret platform fighter floatplanes from capital ships. The type proved to be popular with pilots as they were easy to fly and very manoeuvrable, and they remained in service until 1934 when the last examples, some floatplanes of No.406 flight, were replaced by Hawker Ospreys.

A total of 196 Flycatchers, including prototypes, were produced by Fairey.

Fairey Flycatcher I

First flight: November 28, 1922
Power: Armstrong Siddeley 400hp Jaguar IV two row, 14-cylinder radial engine
Armament: Two fixed forward-firing Vickers 0.303in machine-guns plus up to four 9kg/20lb bombs under wings
Size: Wingspan – 8.84m/29ft
Length – 7.01m/23ft
Height – 3.66m/12ft
Wing area – 26.76m²/288sq ft
Weights: Empty – 9,24kg/2,038lb
Maximum take-off – 1,372kg/3,028lb
Performance: Maximum speed – 216kph/134mph
Ceiling – 5,790m/19,000ft
Range – 500km/311 miles
Climb – 3,050m/10,000ft in 9 minutes, 29 seconds

ABOVE: **Float-equipped Flycatchers would be fired off rails like this from Royal Navy ships to carry out reconnaissance duties and extend the ship's eyes over the horizon.**

Fairey Fulmar

The Fleet Air Arm, keen to update its fighter fleet in the late 1930s, nevertheless severely limited designers' imagination by insisting that any new FAA fighter had to be a two-seater. It was felt that the pilot's workload would have been too great, had he needed to focus on controlling the aircraft at the same time as keeping it on course using the new complex navigational aids.

Fairey's proposal was what became the Fulmar, a two-seat reconnaissance fighter developed from their P.4/34 light bomber design. The Fulmar looked very similar to Fairey's Battle but was in fact smaller and lighter – its performance, however, was not much more impressive as the two-seat configuration increased weight thus affecting speed, climb and ceiling. It was clear that the Fulmar was inferior to contemporary single-seat

fighters, but it was tough and reliable and packed the same firepower as the RAF's Spitfires and Hurricanes.

The prototype first flew on January 4, 1940, at Ringway (now Manchester International Airport) and 159 production aircraft had been produced for the Fleet Air Arm by the end of the year. The first front-line FAA unit to receive the type was No.806 in June 1940, and in August 1940 the squadron boarded HMS *Illustrious*.

Fulmars fought from the Arctic to the Far East – they defended convoys, took part in attacks on enemy warships and the invasions of North Africa and Sicily, defended Malta and Ceylon, and shot down many enemy aircraft, some of them while serving as night-fighters.

With the Fleet Air Arm in action in the Pacific as well as in European waters the FAA simply had to acquire truly modern carrier-based fighters so the Fulmar was gradually replaced by the Supermarine Seafire in 1943. The type did, however, continue to fly in secondary roles including the training of Barracuda crews.

The Fulmar ultimately equipped 19 Fleet Air Arm squadrons and 1 RAF unit. Of the 601 Fulmars built, only one remains, preserved by the Fleet Air Arm Museum in the UK. This aircraft is N1854, the prototype Fulmar which was the first and is now the last of the type.

LEFT: Crews found the Fulmar comparatively pleasant to fly, and its wide undercarriage track, evident in this photograph, meant it was a good carrier deck aircraft.

Fairey Fulmar I

First flight: January 4, 1940
Power: One Rolls-Royce 1,080hp Merlin VIII engine
Armament: Eight wing-mounted 0.303in machine-guns and one 0.303in machine-gun in rear cockpit
Size: Wingspan – 14.13m/46ft 5in
Length – 12.27m/40ft 3in
Height – 4.27m/14ft
Wing area – 31.77m²/342sq ft
Weights: Empty – 3,187kg/7,026lb
Maximum take-off – 4,445kg/9,800lb
Performance: Maximum speed – 450kph/280mph
Ceiling – 7,925m/26,000ft
Range – 1,287km/800 miles
Climb – 366m/1,200ft per minute

LEFT: **A Fairey Swordfish prepares to catch the wire. Note the extended arrester hook and the rails beneath the wings for carrying eight 27kg/60lb rockets.**
BELOW: **Swordfish ranged on a carrier deck waiting for the order to prepare to launch. The Swordfish was a tough aircraft.**

Fairey Swordfish

The Fairey Swordfish holds a remarkable place in aviation history as it is one of the few combat aircraft to have been operational at both the start and end of World War II. This rugged aircraft was also the last British military biplane in front-line service and had the distinction of serving longer than the aircraft intended to replace it in Fleet Air Arm service. The 'Stringbag' was developed from an earlier failed Fairey design and first flew in April 1934 designated TSR II (Torpedo Spotter Reconnaissance II).

After successful service trials, a contract to supply 86 Swordfish Mk Is to the Royal Navy's Fleet Air Arm was signed. The Swordfish entered service with No.825 Squadron in July 1936 and over the next three years a further 600 aircraft were delivered, equipping 13 Fleet Air Arm squadrons. During World

War II another 12 squadrons were formed and equipped with the venerable biplane.

The wartime exploits of this deceptively frail-looking aircraft are legendary. Its first major action was against the Italian naval base at Taranto on November 11, 1940. HMS *Illustrious* launched 21 Swordfish of Nos.815 and 819 Squadrons to make a night attack on the Italian fleet. During the raid the Swordfish destroyed three battleships, two destroyers, a cruiser and other smaller ships for the loss of only two of the attacking aircraft. The attack crippled the Italian fleet and eliminated the opportunity for Italian warships to bolster German naval strength in the Mediterranean.

Other notable actions include the crippling of the German battleship *Bismarck* in May 1941. Swordfish from the Royal Navy carriers HMS *Victorious* and HMS *Ark Royal* were involved in the search for the German battleship. The first Swordfish attack, led by Lieutenant Commander Esmonde, was launched from *Victorious* but none of the torpedoes from the nine aircraft caused serious damage. During the second attack, delivered by 20 Swordfish from the *Ark Royal*, a torpedo severely damaged *Bismarck*'s rudder, greatly limiting the ship's manoeuvrability. The pursuing British task force were then able to catch and finally sink *Bismarck* with naval gunfire.

ABOVE: **A fine air-to-air study of a Swordfish formation. Note the 18in torpedo on the aircraft in the foreground. Note also the bomb shackles beneath the wings that could carry an alternative warload to the 'tin fish'.**

LEFT: **During World War II, Swordfish accounted for the sinking of over 300,000 tons of Axis shipping so were a major contribution towards the Allied victory in the Battle of the Atlantic and in gaining naval supremacy in the Mediterranean.** ABOVE: **The Royal Navy Historic Flight maintains two of these remarkable aircraft in airworthy condition – a Mk I and a Mk II.**

In February 1942, crews of No.825 Squadron carried out a gallant attack against the *Scharnhorst, Gneisenau* and *Prinz Eugen* during which all six aircraft were shot down. Only five of the 18 crew members survived. For his bravery and leadership under fire, Lieutenant Commander Esmonde, veteran of the *Bismarck* mission, and leader of the attack, was posthumously awarded the Victoria Cross, the highest British and Commonwealth military award for gallantry.

While the Mk I was an all-metal fabric covered aircraft, the Mk II Swordfish, which entered service in 1943, had metal-clad lower wings to enable the aircraft to fire rocket projectiles without setting fire to the previously fabric-covered wings. Later the same year ASV (air-to-surface-vessel) radar was installed between the aircraft's fixed undercarriage legs on Mk IIIs while the Mk IV had an enclosed cockpit.

During the desperate Battle of the Atlantic, there were simply not enough aircraft carriers to escort Allied convoys across the ocean. As a stopgap measure to provide some protection for the convoys, Britain converted grain ships and oil tankers to become MAC (Merchant Aircraft Carrier) ships. Grain ships, fitted with a 123m/400ft flight deck, a below-deck hangar and lift, operated four Swordfish. The tankers had a 140m/460ft flight deck but no hangar in which to accommodate their three Swordfish – the MAC Swordfish suffered considerable wear and tear.

In the closing weeks of the war, the Royal Air Force operated a small number of all-black Mk III Swordfish – equipped with ASV radar and operating from landing strips in Belgium, these aircraft were tasked with the destruction of German submarines off the Dutch coast.

From 1940, all development and production of the venerable Swordfish passed from Fairey to the Blackburn Aircraft Company, which built 1,699 (unofficially known as 'Blackfish') of the 2,391 aircraft produced in total.

ABOVE: **Three Swordfish at the time of D-Day in 1944 wearing hastily-applied identification stripes. There were not many biplanes in front-line service at D-Day but the Swordfish was there.**

Fairey Swordfish Mk I

First flight: April 17, 1934
Power: One Bristol 690hp Pegasus IIIM3 9-cylinder air-cooled radial engine
Armament: One fixed 0.303in Browning machine-gun in the nose and one flexible 0.303in Vickers or Lewis machine-gun in the rear cockpit, one 45cm/18in 730kg/1,610lb torpedo or one 680kg/1,500lb mine or bombs
Size: Wingspan – 13.87m/45ft 6in
Length – 10.87m/35ft 8in
Height – 3.76m/12ft 4in
Wing area – 56.39m²/607sq ft
Weights: Empty – 2,132kg/4,700lb
Maximum take-off – 3,407kg/7,510lb
Performance: Maximum speed – 222kph/138mph
Service ceiling – 5,029m/16,500ft
Range – 1,658km/1,030 miles unloaded
Climb – 3,048m/10,000ft in 15 minutes, 2 seconds

LEFT: **While operating from German Navy ships in search of enemy craft, the Fl 282 was setting the foundations for the use of helicopters as naval weapons.** ABOVE: **This prototype was fitted with a largely glazed nose. Note the searchlight under the nose.**

Flettner Fl 282

The Fl 282 *Kolibri* (Hummingbird) was developed by German aeronautical scientist and helicopter pioneer Anton Flettner. Having built his first helicopter in 1930, Flettner produced the Fl 265 that first flew in 1939 and from this developed the Fl 282, designed from the outset for military use. Intended to carry a pilot and an observer, the design was judged to have so much potential for naval use that no fewer than 30 prototypes and 15 pre-production machines were ordered simultaneously to accelerate development and production. The pilot sat in front of the rotors in a typically open cockpit while the observer sat in a single compartment aft of the rotors, facing backwards.

Small, fast and agile, in mock attacks Luftwaffe fighter pilots found it hard to

keep the small helicopter in their gunsights. The *Kolibri* could land on a ship, even in heavy seas. Mass production was ordered but Allied bombing of the factories meant that only the prototypes were produced. Nevertheless it was 24 of these aircraft that entered service with the German Navy in 1943 for escort service, flying off the gun turrets of ships to spot submarines, and performing resupply missions in even the worst weather conditions. The Fl 282 was designed so the rotor blades and landing gear could be removed and the helicopter could be stored on a U-boat, although it is not known if this happened. This pioneering military helicopter served in the Baltic, North Aegean and the Mediterranean.

In the clear blue water of the Mediterranean the Fl 282 could spot a submerged submarine as deep as 40m/130ft, mark the enemy's position with a smoke bomb, then radio the position to its home ship while shadowing the submarine – this was groundbreaking use of the helicopter for anti-submarine warfare.

Only three of these helicopters survived the war as the rest of the fleet were destroyed to prevent their capture by the Allies. Two of the surviving machines went to the United States and Britain while the third ended up in the Soviet Union. Anton Flettner moved to the United States after the War and became an adviser to the US military.

LEFT: **The pioneering Flettner machines are often overlooked in aviation history, but the aircraft were true trailblazers. Operational by 1942 on German warships in the Baltic, Mediterranean and Aegean, the type was effectively the world's first military helicopter.**

Flettner Fl 282	

First flight: 1941
Power: One Bramo 160hp Sh 14A radial
  piston engine
Armament: None
Size: Rotor diameter – 11.96m/39ft 2.75in
  Length – 6.56m/21ft 6.25in
  Height – 2.2m/7ft 2.5in
Weights: Empty – 760kg/1,676lb
  Maximum take-off – 1,000kg/2,205lb
Performance: Maximum speed – 150kph/93mph
  Ceiling – 3,300m/10,825ft
  Range – 170km/106 miles
  Climb – 91.5m/300ft per minute

Focke-Achgelis Fa 330

The Focke-Achgelis Fa 330 *Bachstelze* (Wagtail) was a simple and unusual flying machine – a rotary kite. World War II German submarines sat low in the water and the crew could not see more than a few miles around so they were always at risk from fast-moving enemy destroyers. The Fa 330 was a solution developed to be towed on a winched cable in the air behind U-boats to extend their range of vision. By mid-1942, sea trials proved that the Fa 330 could work but only the Type IX U-boat could tow the Fa 330 fast enough for flight in low wind conditions.

The airframe consisted of two 6.35cm/2.5in diameter steel tubes forming an inverted T. While one tube was the 'fuselage' of the aircraft with the pilot's seat and instruments (altimeter, airspeed indicator and tachometer), the other tube served as the rotor mast. A control stick hung from the rotor blade hub and the pilot simply moved the stick for direct pitch and roll control and used foot pedals to move the large rudder to control yaw. The rotor blades consisted of a steel spar supporting plywood ribs skinned with fabric-covered plywood.

When not assembled, the Fa 330 was stored in two long watertight compartments built into the U-boat's conning tower. One tube contained the

blades and tail and the other contained the fuselage. In calm conditions, four crewmen could assemble the entire aircraft on the deck of the submarine in just three minutes.

As the U-boat sped along, the airflow would begin to spin the rotors resulting in autorotation, the movement of relative wind up through the rotor blades which caused them to turn with enough speed to generate lift and carry the craft aloft without an engine. To speed up take-off, a deckhand could pull hard on a rope wrapped around a drum on the rotor hub to spin the rotor.

The craft would be towed by a cable around 150m/492ft long and 'fly' about 120m/393ft above the surface where visibility was 25 nautical miles compared to just 5 nautical miles from the conning tower of a U-boat. Normal flight revolutions per minute (rpm) were about 205rpm at a standard towing airspeed of 40kph/25mph while a minimum speed of 27kph/17mph was required to maintain autorotation. The pilot talked to the submarine using an intercom system via a wire wrapped around the towing cable.

In the event of an attack that would cause the U-boat to dive, both the pilot and craft were expendable although he was equipped with a parachute. Allied

air-cover was so good in the North Atlantic that only U-boats operating in the far southern parts of the Atlantic and the Indian Ocean deployed the Fa 330. Use of the Fa 330 assisted U-boat *U-177* to intercept and sink the Greek steamer *Eithalia Mari* on August 6, 1943.

Several are preserved in museums around the world.

Focke-Achgelis Fa 330	

First flight: 1942
Power: None
Armament: None
Size: Rotor diameter – 7.32m/24ft
  Length – 4.42m/14ft 6in
  Height – 1.7m/5ft 6in
Weights: Empty – 68kg/150lb
Performance: Airspeed between 27kph/17mph and 40kph/25mph to maintain flight

LEFT: **N5513 was a Sea Gladiator I that served in Alexandria and with HMS** *Eagle* **before being lost on Crete in May 1941.** ABOVE: **Sea Gladiator N5519, better known as** *Charity* **of Malta's Hal Far Fighter Flight, one of** *Faith, Hope* **and** *Charity.*

Gloster Sea Gladiator

The Gloster Gladiator was the RAF's last biplane fighter, and entered service in February 1937, by which time it was already obsolete. Although largely replaced by the start of World War II, the Gladiators of Nos.607 and 615 Auxiliary Squadrons were deployed to France with the Air Component of the Allied Expeditionary Force in November 1939. The squadrons were converting to Spitfires and Hurricanes when the German attack in the West was launched in May 1940, and the Gladiators proved to be no match for the modern Luftwaffe fighters.

The Gladiator had caught the eye of the Admiralty who ordered 60 fully navalized Sea Gladiators. The Sea Gladiator differed from the land-based version, Gladiator Mk II, by being fitted with an arrester hook for deck landings, catapult points for deck launches, and carrying a collapsible dinghy beneath a ventral fairing under the fuselage between the undercarriage legs.

It was Gladiator Mk I K6129 on loan from the RAF that undertook aircraft carrier trials with No.800 Squadron during the summer of 1938 on board HMS *Furious*. As an interim replacement for the Hawker Ospreys and Nimrods the Sea Gladiator was to replace, 38 RAF Gladiator Mk IIs were fitted with arrester hooks for carrier operations and were transferred to the Fleet Air Arm from December 1938 while the fully navalized Sea Gladiators were being developed.

By the start of World War II the carrier-borne Sea Gladiators were, like their land-based cousins, obsolete. The first deliveries had taken place in 1938 with the first Sea Gladiator unit being No.769 Squadron, a training unit. The Navy's first operational Sea Gladiator unit (November 1939) was No.804 Squadron.

It is, however, for the glorious defence of a beleaguered Malta that the Sea Gladiator is best known. From the

aircraft of No.802 Squadron that remained at Malta following the sinking of HMS *Glorious* in 1940, three Sea Gladiators became international legends. *Faith, Hope* and *Charity* were part of the Hal Far Fighter Flight, composed of both RAF and FAA personnel. In June 1940, *Faith* alone destroyed two Italian bombers within 24 hours.

Elsewhere, Sea Gladiators undertook less hazardous duties as faster fighter aircraft types entered front-line service. However, the type remained in use until 1944, employed in secondary roles, including communications, liaison and meteorological reconnaissance.

Gloster Sea Gladiator Mk II

First flight: September 12, 1934 (Gladiator prototype)
Power: Bristol 840hp Mercury VIIIA air-cooled radial piston engine
Armament: Two 0.303in machine-guns in nose plus two more mounted in wing
Size: Wingspan – 9.83m/32ft 3in
Length – 8.36m/27ft 5in
Height – 3.15m/10ft 4in
Wing area – 30.01m²/323sq ft
Weights: Empty – 1,692kg/3,730lb
Maximum take-off – 2,449kg/5,400lb
Performance: Maximum speed – 392kph/244mph
Ceiling – 9,700m/31,825ft
Range – 680km/423 miles
Climb – 6,095m/20,000ft in 9 minutes, 30 seconds

ABOVE: **Having first entered Royal Navy service in 1938, the Sea Gladiator continued to serve until 1944 in secondary roles. In all, 60 aircraft were supplied to the FAA.**

LEFT: **Grumman's F2F was nicknamed the 'flying barrel' for reasons clear in this port-side view. Note the recess that housed the undercarriage when it was raised.** ABOVE: **The clearance between the top of the fuselage and the upper wing was negligible, so the pilot usually had to look over the wing instead when in the air.**

Grumman F2F-1

Grumman's long association with the US Navy and reputation as naval aircraft specialists began in March 1931 when the US Navy ordered a prototype two-seat biplane fighter, the XFF-1. The all-metal XFF-1 had a top speed of 314kph/195mph and was faster than the US Navy's standard fighter of the time, the Boeing F4B-4.

The Navy ordered the Grumman biplane and it entered USN service as the FF-1 from April 1933. Canadian licence-built versions known as Goblins were supplied to the RCAF and single examples went to Nicaragua and Japan. Spanish Republican forces also acquired 40 aircraft and the two-seaters were in action against Spanish Nationalist forces between 1936–39.

The FF-1 was clearly a fine design and Grumman inevitably began to develop a single-seat version which became the F2F-1. The single-seater was lighter than the FF-1, had a top speed of 383kph/238mph and entered US Navy service during 1935, replacing the F4B. The F2F-1, known as the 'flying barrel', remained in front-line service aboard USS *Lexington* until as late as September 1940 at which point it became an advanced trainer.

The F2F-1 had exhibited some inherent directional instability which Grumman sought to eradicate in an improved design, the F3F. With a longer fuselage and wings, together with other aerodynamic refinements, the F3F-1 prototype first flew in March 1935 but

crashed two days later killing the pilot when the engine and wings detached themselves from the fuselage in a test dive. Wing and engine fittings were strengthened on the second prototype which itself crashed on May 17 after the pilot was unable to recover from a flat spin. Remarkably, the crashed aircraft was rebuilt and was back in the air after just three weeks, fitted with a small ventral fin beneath the tail to aid spin recovery. The F3F-1 entered US Navy service aboard USS *Ranger* and *Saratoga* in 1936. US Marine Corps unit VMF-211 was the last to retire the F3F in October 1941 – by which point it was the last biplane fighter in US service.

LEFT: **The Grumman fighter was popular when it joined the US Fleet, but as a biplane entering service in the mid-1930s, its time in the front line was limited.**

Grumman F2F-1	

First flight: October 18, 1933
Power: Pratt & Whitney 650hp R-1535-72 Twin Wasp Junior radial piston engine
Armament: Two 0.3in machine-guns
Size: Wingspan – 8.69m/28ft 6in
　　　Length – 6.53m/21ft 5in
　　　Height – 2.77m/9ft 1in
　　　Wing area – 21.37m²/230sq ft
Weights: Empty – 1,221kg/2,691lb
　　　Maximum take-off – 1,745kg/3,847lb
Performance: Maximum speed – 383kph/238mph
　　　Ceiling – 8,380m/27,500ft
　　　Range – 1,585km/985 miles
　　　Climb – 939m/3,080ft per minute

Grumman Avenger

Grumman's large single-engine torpedo-bomber was patriotically and appropriately named Avenger on December 7, 1941, the 'Day of Infamy' on which Japan attacked Pearl Harbor. Procured and constructed in great quantities, the Avenger saw action with Allied air arms in virtually all theatres of operation in World War II. Of the 9,836 aircraft produced, 2,290 were built by Grumman (so somewhat confusingly designated TBF) while the General Motors Eastern Division produced the rest which were TBMs, the designation by which all Avengers are sometimes erroneously known.

The Avenger was first flown on August 1, 1941, having been designed in just five weeks – an incredible feat by today's standards when computer-aided designs can take a decade to perfect. The aircraft, designed for a three-man crew, had an internal weapons bay to minimize drag, gun turret, and a rear defensive gun position. A hatch on the right side rear of the wing allowed access into the rear fuselage which was packed with equipment, flares, parachutes and ammunition. On the

ABOVE: The Avenger was a large, well-armed and hard-hitting carrier-borne warplane that, despite a poor combat debut, made a key contribution to the Allied victory in World War II.

lower level, the bombardier had a folding seat from which he could either man the lower rear machine-gun, or face forward and aim the aircraft for medium-altitude level bombing. The pilot sat in a roomy and comfortable cockpit above the wing's leading edge and enjoyed excellent visibility.

Only one aircraft returned from the six that made the Avenger's combat debut at Midway in June 1942. Despite this poor start, the Avenger went on to become one of the great naval combat aircraft of World War II, being involved in the destruction of more than 60 Japanese warships. It was the first US single-engined aircraft able to carry the hard-hitting 22in torpedo (as well as depth charges, rockets and bombs) and was also the first to boast a power-operated gun turret. Torpedoes launched by US Navy Avengers were largely

LEFT: The Avenger became the standard US Navy torpedo-bomber of World War II, and numbered among its pilots a young naval aviator who went on to become President George Herbert Bush. ABOVE: In Royal Navy service the Avenger was at first called Tarpon, but was later redesignated Avenger.

LEFT: **These three Avengers were flying with No.846 Fleet Air Arm when they were photographed in December 1943.** ABOVE: **Even with its folding wings the Avenger was still a large aircraft, due partly to its large internal weapons bay. Ordnance could also be carried externally.**

responsible for the sinking of the large Japanese battleships *Yamato* and *Musashi*.

The Royal Navy received 402 Avengers (designated TBF-1Bs), under the Anglo-American Lend-Lease arrangement – the first unit, No.832 Squadron (on board HMS *Victorious*) being equipped in early 1943. Although originally designated Tarpon Mk Is for British service, they were later redesignated Avenger Mk Is.

Around 330 TBM-1s were also supplied to the Royal Navy and designated Avenger Mk IIs. Delivery of the TBM-3 began in April 1944 with the Royal Navy receiving the 222 TBM-3 aircraft which were designated Avenger Mk III by the British. Torpedo-bomber versions remained in RN service until 1947 and then in 1953, the Royal Navy began acquiring anti-submarine versions designated the Avenger AS Mk IV or AS Mk V. The Avenger finally retired from the Royal Navy in 1962 after almost two decades of service.

In 1951, Royal Canadian Navy anti-submarine units were re-equipped with wartime Avengers, which had been overhauled and updated. In 1955, a further eight Avengers entered Canadian service in the Airborne Early Warning role.

Also during World War II, New Zealand acquired two squadrons of Grumman Avengers which were used as dive bombers by Nos.30 and 31 Squadrons. Secondary roles undertaken by the Kiwi Avengers included target drogue towing and, incredibly, the spraying of Japanese vegetable plots with diesel oil.

Post-war, the type was also adapted to a wide variety of civilian uses including crop-spraying and water-bombing. In New Zealand during 1947 an Avenger was used for trials of aerial seed-sowing and fertilizing. With an additional auxiliary fuel tank converted into a hopper installed in the 'bomb bay', it could carry 1,017kg/2,240lb of fertilizer. A few examples remain in flying condition in Britain and the USA.

ABOVE: **This preserved TBM-3R, with its rear turret position glazed over, was developed to carry seven passengers or cargo on to carriers. The US Navy needed a carrier-capable aircraft for the cargo role, and the tough Avenger was perfect. It removed the need to develop a role-specific type.**

Grumman TBM-3 Avenger

First flight: August 1, 1941
Power: One Wright 1,900hp R-2600-20 radial
Armament: Two 0.50in fixed forward-firing machine-guns in the upper part of the forward fuselage; two trainable 0.30in machine-guns in rear cockpit; external bomb or depth-charge load of 1,021kg/2,250lb
Size: Wingspan – 16.51m/54ft 2in
Length – 12.48m/40ft 11in
Height – 5m/16ft 5in
Wing area – 45.52m^2/490sq ft
Weights: Empty – 47,83kg/10,545lb
Maximum take-off – 8,117kg/17,895lb
Performance: Maximum speed – 444kph/276mph
Service ceiling – 7,620km/25,000ft
Range – 1,609km/1,000 miles
Climb – 328m/1,075ft per minute

Grumman F4F Wildcat

With its wing set midway up its stubby fuselage, the Wildcat looks like a biplane missing a set of wings. There is a good reason for that – it was originally conceived as a biplane but was redesigned as a monoplane, the F4F, in 1936. Its industrial appearance, due to the entirely riveted fuselage, masked an aircraft with excellent speed and manoeuvrability.

In early 1939 the French Aéronavale placed the first order for the type with Grumman and this was followed in August that year by an order from the US Navy. After France fell, aircraft destined for the Aéronavale were diverted to Britain where the first examples for Britain's Fleet Air Arm arrived in July 1940. This fascinating time in the Wildcat's history is often overlooked by historians. The British named the F4F the Martlet and put the type into service almost immediately with No.804 Squadron in the Orkneys. In December 1940, two of these Martlets became the first US-built fighters in British

ABOVE: **Despite having first flown in 1937, the Wildcat was still in the front line and winning dogfights until the end of World War II.**

World War II service to destroy a German aircraft. In September 1941, No.802 Squadron became the first FAA unit to go to sea with Martlets, aboard HMS *Audacity*, and on the 20th of the month, two of the aircraft shot down a Focke-Wulf 200 that was shadowing their convoy. Martlets of the Royal Naval Fighter Unit saw action over the Western Desert and shot down an Italian Fiat G.50 on September 28, 1941.

In May 1942, over Madagascar, FAA Martlets saw action against Vichy French aircraft and in August that year during a convoy to Malta, they tackled Italian bombers over the Mediterranean. By now the Martlet/Wildcat was known as a formidable fighter aircraft. Pilots praised its destructive firepower but knew it was a tricky aircraft to fly and handle on the ground too.

ABOVE: **Retaining the semi-recessed undercarriage-up arrangement of earlier Grumman types, the Wildcat was derived from a biplane design.**

ABOVE: **The Fleet Air Arm was first to put the Wildcat into combat as the Martlet Mk I. The aircraft got its first 'kills' in December 1940.**

LEFT: The Wildcat was an excellent carrier-borne fighter – small, tough, durable and hard to outmanoeuvre in combat. BELOW: The Wildcat was one of the Fleet Air Arm's primary naval fighters until Wildcat squadrons started to be re-equipped with either the Hellcat or Corsair during 1943. However, many remained in service with the FAA until 1946.

When the USA entered World War II in December 1941, the F4F, by now known as the Wildcat, was the most widely used fighter on US aircraft carriers and also equipped many land-based US Marine Corps squadrons. This tough, hard-hitting and highly manoeuvrable aircraft was the US Navy's only carrier-borne fighter until the 1943 arrival of the Hellcat. Wildcats were central to some of the war's most remarkable heroic actions involving US Navy and USMC pilots.

Marine Corps Wildcats operated extensively from land bases, one of which was Henderson Field on Guadalcanal and it was from here that the Americans mounted their first offensive action of the war in the Pacific. One USMC Wildcat pilot, Captain Joe Foss, a flight commander with Marine Fighting Squadron VMF-121, led his flight of eight Wildcats from Guadalcanal to 72 confirmed aerial victories in a matter of 16 weeks. Foss himself shot down a total of 26 Japanese aircraft, including 5 in a single day, and was awarded the Medal of Honor.

Although in a straight fight Wildcats could not cope well with a Japanese Zero, the Grumman fighter's armour plating and self-sealing fuel tanks together with its pilot's tenacity made it a potent adversary in a dogfight. US Navy Wildcats were phased out in favour of the Grumman Hellcat in late 1943 but Britain's Fleet Air Arm continued to operate the Wildcat until the end of the war. In March 1945, Wildcats (the British abandoned the name Martlet in January 1944) of No.882 Squadron destroyed four Messerschmitt Bf109s over Norway in what was the FAA's last wartime victory over German fighters.

Wildcats manufactured by General Motors were designated FM-1 and -2.

ABOVE: The unusual paint scheme applied to this preserved Wildcat by the US-based Commemorative Air Force did not please the purists but it does remind air show audiences of the type's distinguished FAA service.

Grumman FM-2 Wildcat

First flight: March 1943 (FM-2)
Power: Wright Cyclone 1,350hp R-1820-56 9-cylinder air-cooled radial
Armament: Six 0.5in machine-guns in outer wings plus two underwing 113kg/250lb bombs or six 5in rockets
Size: Wingspan – 11.58m/38ft
Length – 8.80m/28ft 11in
Height – 3.50m/11ft 5in
Wing area – 24.16m²/260sq ft
Weights: Empty – 2,223kg/4,900lb
Maximum take-off – 3,362kg/7,412lb
Performance: Maximum speed – 534kph/332mph
Service ceiling – 10,576m/34,700ft
Range – 1,448km/900 miles
Climb – 610m/2,000ft per minute

Grumman F6F Hellcat

Rightly described as a war-winning naval aircraft, the F6F Hellcat was developed from the F4F Wildcat. Designed and produced in record time, the Hellcat's combat debut in August 1943 firmly swung the air power balance of the war in the Pacific in favour of the United States. From then on, all the major Pacific air battles were dominated by the F6F. In its first big air battle, in the Kwajalein area on December 4, 1943, 91 Hellcats fought 50 Japanese A6M Zeros and destroyed 28 for the loss of only 2. Powered by the Pratt & Whitney R-2800 Double Wasp, the robust Hellcat was credited with 75 per cent of all enemy aircraft destroyed by US Navy carrier pilots with an overall F6F kills to losses ratio in excess of 19:1. The Hellcat was America's all-time top 'ace-making' aircraft with no less than 307 pilots credited with the destruction of five or more enemy aircraft while flying the Grumman fighter. US Navy pilot Lieutenant Bill Hardy became an ace in a day on April 6, 1945, when in a single 70-minute sortie he engaged and destroyed five Japanese aircraft.

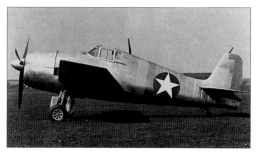

TOP: **The Grumman Hellcat was the aircraft that the Allies could not have done without in the Pacific War but the Hellcat needed the carriers to operate.**
ABOVE: **The XF6F-4 was one of a number of prototype 'Hellcats' used to trial engine and armament installations during the type's development.**

Effective at any altitude, the Hellcat's unusual features included backwards-retracting landing gear and a distinctive 31.13m²/335sq ft wing larger than that of any other major single-engined fighter of World War II. The outer sections of the folding wings each contained three 0.5in machine-guns with 400 rounds each.

Night-fighter versions appeared in early 1944 equipped with radar and ensured that the Hellcats were an ever-present threat to their enemies. The Hellcat omnipresence in Pacific combat zones night or day came to be known as 'The Big Blue Blanket'. US Navy ace Lt Alex Vraciu destroyed 19 Japanese aircraft while flying Hellcats, 6 of them in one spectacular 8-minute engagement, and later described the F6F as "...tough, hardhitting, dependable – one hell of an airplane."

From April 1943, Britain's Fleet Air Arm received 252 F6F-3s under the Lend-Lease programme. Initially renamed the Gannet

ABOVE: **The Grumman Hellcat was fast and well armed, and was able to claim over 5,000 enemy aircraft destroyed by the end of World War II.**

LEFT: **Over 2,500 Hellcats were built during 1943 alone and even the mighty Corsair was not able to displace Grumman's fighter from front-line service.**
ABOVE RIGHT: **The Hellcat was developed with the benefit of air combat experience in both the Pacific and European Theatres.** BELOW: **The all-metal Hellcat had flush-riveted skin and was powered by a mighty 2,000hp Pratt & Whitney engine that helped it outpace enemy aircraft.**

in Royal Navy service, British F6Fs saw a lot of combat in actions off Norway, in the Mediterranean and the Far East, including the final assault on Japan. By late 1945 the Hellcat had been almost completely replaced in Royal Navy service, although a senior Fleet Air Arm officer is known to have had a personal F6F until 1953.

When the last aircraft rolled off the production line in November 1945 it made a total Hellcat production figure of 12,272, 11,000 of which were built in just two years. Swift production of the Hellcat has been attributed to the soundness of the original design, which required few engineering changes while production was underway.

Other nations that operated the Hellcat included France whose Aéronavale used them in Indochina, while the Argentine and Uruguayan navies used them until 1961.

Some US Navy Hellcats were converted into drones packed with explosives and in August 1952, six of these remotely controlled F6F-5Ks were directed on to North Korean targets.

ABOVE: **The Hellcat was for many the ultimate naval fighter of World War II, but the type flew on in front-line service with some air arms into the 1950s and saw action in Korea and Indochina.**

Grumman F6F-5 Hellcat

First flight: June 26, 1942
Power: Pratt & Whitney 2,000hp R-2800-10W 18-cylinder two-row air-cooled radial piston engine
Armament: Six 0.5in Browning machine-guns, plus provision for bombs up to 907kg/2,000lb
Size: Wingspan – 13m/42ft 10in
  Length – 10.2m/33ft 7in
  Height – 3.96m/13ft
  Wing area – 31m²/334sq ft
Weights: Empty – 4,152kg/9,153lb
  Maximum take-off – 6,991kg/15,413lb
Performance: Maximum speed – 621kph/386mph
  Ceiling – 11,369m/37,300ft
  Range – 1,674km/1,040 miles on internal fuel
  Climb – 1,039m/3,410ft per minute

LEFT: **The Bearcat was considered by many to be the ultimate piston-powered fighter with a performance to rival any land-based aircraft of the time and even that of the early jets.**
BELOW LEFT: **The Bearcat arrived too late for World War II service but was produced until 1949.**

Grumman F8F Bearcat

The Bearcat was the last in the Grumman series of carrier-based fighters that had started back in 1931 with the Grumman FF. It was one of the fastest piston-engined aircraft ever and was built to a US Navy specification calling for a small, light, high-performance naval interceptor.

Grumman's design team aimed to create the diminutive high-performance fighter around the mighty Pratt & Whitney R-2800 Double Wasp that had been used to power Grumman's Hellcat and Tigercat. The Bearcat was 20 per cent lighter than the Hellcat and had a 30 per cent greater rate of climb than its Grumman stablemate as well as being 80kph/50mph faster.

Many features of the Bearcat's design were reportedly inspired by a captured Luftwaffe Focke-Wulf Fw 190 fighter that had been handed over to Grumman. The Bearcat's large 3.76m/12ft 4in four-bladed propeller required long landing gear which gave the Bearcat its characteristic nose-up attitude on the ground. It was also the first US Navy aircraft with a bubble canopy that afforded a clear view for the pilot in all directions. These factors, together with its excellent manoeuvrability and good low-level performance, made it an outstanding fighter aircraft in all respects.

The F8F prototypes were ordered in November 1943 and the type first took to the air on August 21, 1944, only nine months later. The first production aircraft (the F8F-1) were delivered in February 1945, a mere six months after the prototype test flight.

In May 1945, US Navy Fighter Squadron VF-19 became the first unit to equip with the Bearcat and was operational by May 21, 1945, but the type arrived too late to see action in World War II. It is worth noting that in comparative trials at this time, the Bearcat's impressive performance allowed it to outmanoeuvre most of the early jet fighters.

Production nevertheless continued until May 1949 by which time 24 US Navy squadrons were operating Bearcats including the US Navy's Blue Angels team who had re-equipped with the F8F-1 Bearcat on August 25, 1946 – the team used Bearcats until its temporary disbandment during the Korean War in 1950.

The F8F-1B version (100 built), was armed with four 20mm cannon instead of the four 0.5in machine-guns of the F8F-1. Almost 300 examples of the F8F-2 were built with 20mm cannon armament as standard. Radar-equipped night-fighter and photo-reconnaissance versions were also made in small numbers.

Grumman's F9F Panther and the McDonnell F2H Banshee largely replaced the Bearcat in US Navy service, as their performance finally overtook that of piston-engine fighters.

LEFT: **The Hellcat remained in service well after the end of World War II, peaking with its equipping of 24 post-war US Navy units.** ABOVE: **The type was withdrawn from service by late 1952, replaced by jets like the Banshee and Panther.**

The Bearcat was phased out of front-line US Navy use by 1952 but around 250 were refurbished and sold as F8F-1Ds to the French Armée de l'Air who used them in action in Indochina. Many of these aircraft were later acquired by the air forces of both North and South Vietnam. The Royal Thai Air Force were also supplied with about 130 Bearcats.

In 1946, a standard production F8F-1 set a time-to-climb record (after a run of only 35m/115ft) of 3,050m/10,000ft in 94 seconds. The Bearcat held this record for ten years until it was broken by a jet fighter which was nonetheless unable to beat the Bearcat's incredibly short take-off run.

The 1946 record-breaking feat led to another career for the Bearcat – air racing. A standard Bearcat won the first of the famous Reno Air Races in 1964, then *Rare Bear*, a highly modified F8F, dominated the air racing scene for decades. *Rare Bear* also set many performance records, including the 3km/1.9-mile world speed record for piston-driven aircraft of 850.26kph/528.33mph in 1989.

In 1972, this souped-up Bearcat had set a new time-to-climb record of 3,000m/9,843ft in 91.9 seconds, breaking the record set by the 1946 Bearcat.

ABOVE: **In service the Bearcat would typically fly with a 150-US gallon droppable auxiliary fuel tank under its centreline to extend its range.** LEFT: **This Bearcat is one of a number of examples of the high-performance Grumman fighter maintained in flying condition either for air racing or for air show participation. Note the long undercarriage legs essential to keep the propeller clear of a pitching carrier deck on landing.**

Grumman F8F-1B Bearcat

First flight: August 21, 1944
Power: Pratt & Whitney 2,100hp R-2800-34W Double Wasp 18-cylinder radial piston engine
Armament: Four 20mm cannon plus provision for two 454kg/1,000lb bombs or four 5in rockets under wings
Size: Wingspan – 10.92m/35ft 10in
Length – 8.61m/28ft 3in
Height 4.2m/13ft 10in
Wing area – 22.67m²/244sq ft
Weights: Empty – 3,206kg/7,070lb
Maximum take-off – 5,873kg/12,947lb
Performance: Maximum speed – 677kph/421mph
Ceiling – 11,795m/38,700ft
Range – 1,778km/1,105 miles
Climb – 1,395m/4,570ft per minute

LEFT: **A rare surviving example of a Sea Hurricane. This IB is preserved in the UK in flying condition by The Shuttleworth Collection. The aircraft was built in Canada as a Hurricane I and was converted in the UK to Sea Hurricane standard.** ABOVE: **A Sea Hurricane on its rocket-powered launch rail on board a merchant ship.**

Hawker Sea Hurricane

The Hawker Sea Hurricane was a variant of the famous Hawker Hurricane land-based fighter developed six years after the Hurricane prototype first flew in November 1935. Comparison of the Sea Hurricane/Hurricane and the earlier Hawker Fury's fuselages explains why the embryonic Hurricane was initially known as the Fury Monoplane. The aircraft that only became known as the Hurricane in June 1936 retained the metal-tube construction with fabric covering used by Hawkers since the late 1920s, and not the more modern and complicated stressed-metal fuselage. Stressed-metal-covered wings became standard after early Hurricane models appeared with fabric-covered wings.

It was during the Battle of Britain in 1940 that the Hurricane earned its place in history, accounting for more enemy aircraft than all other defences, ground and air combined. Popular with pilots, the Hurricane was fast, agile and a steady gun platform that could take a lot of punishment. Pilot visibility was better than the contemporary Spitfires as the nose sloped more steeply from the cockpit to the propeller spinner.

The Royal Navy was keen to acquire the Hurricane to help them fight the Battle of the Atlantic which, in early 1940, saw a steep rise in British shipping losses far from shore, away from land-based air cover.

The 'quick-fix' for this was the development of catapult armed merchantmen (CAM ships) from which a fighter could be catapult-launched if enemy aircraft were suspected to be nearby. Hurricanes converted for this role needed only the addition of catapult spools (there was no need for an arrester hook), and 50 Hurricane Mk I landplanes were modified and designated Sea Hurricane Mk IAs.

The 'Hurricat' was mounted on and launched from a rocket-sled catapult on the ship's bows on what was a one-way flight as the aircraft could not land back on board a ship without a carrier deck. Consequently the pilot had to ditch in the sea as near as possible to friendly ships, hoping to be picked up. CAM ship 'Hurricats' alone claimed six enemy aircraft destroyed in the last five months of 1941 with the first victory coming on August 3, 1941, when Lt R.W.H. Everett,

LEFT: **Hook deployed, this Sea Hurricane is preparing to catch the wire on a carrier deck. The Sea Hurricane provided the Fleet Air Arm with a much needed fighter stopgap to keep German bombers at bay in the Battle of the Atlantic.**

LEFT: **These Packard Merlin 29-engined, Canadian-built Sea Hurricane IIAs were naval conversions of the Hurricane Mk XIIA.** BELOW: **A 'Hurricat' launches from a CAM ship. This was a last resort due to the almost certain loss of the aircraft, risk to the pilot and the very visible rocket flare caused by the launch.**

protecting a convoy en route to Gibraltar, intercepted and destroyed a Luftwaffe Focke-Wulf Fw 200 Condor.

Later versions, such as the Sea Hurricane IB, operated conventionally from aircraft carriers, fitted with catapult spools and an arrester hook for carrier landings. Initially the IBs were operated from MAC ships which were large merchantmen fitted with small carrier decks from which fighter and ASW aircraft could operate. These aircraft were open to the harshest conditions as they were permanently stored on the deck as there were no below-deck hangars.

Fleet Air Arm Sea Hurricanes saw action in many theatres but the type's most famous action was fought during August 1942, when aircraft from 801, 802 and 885 Squadrons aboard the carriers HMS *Indomitable*, HMS *Eagle* and HMS *Victorious*, joined with Fairey Fulmars and Grumman Martlets to protect a vital convoy to Malta, in Operation 'Pedestal'. During three days of almost continuous attack by an Axis force of bombers, torpedo-bombers and escorting fighters, 39 enemy aircraft were destroyed for the loss of 8 British fighters.

Sea Hurricanes also hunted and attacked German submarines – in August 1944, three U-boats were attacked in a two-day period.

During World War II the Fleet Air Arm acquired around 600 Sea Hurricanes, 60 of which were built from scratch as Sea Hurricanes while the remainder were conversions from former RAF Hurricanes.

ABOVE: **For a conversion, the Sea Hurricane fulfilled a difficult role well. The non-navalized aircraft suffered from the elements on the Atlantic crossings but gave a good account of themselves when required.**

Hawker Sea Hurricane IIC

First flight: November 6, 1935 (Hurricane prototype)
Power: One Rolls-Royce 1,280hp Merlin XX piston engine
Armament: Four 20mm cannon
Size: Wingspan – 12.19m/40ft
    Length – 9.83m/32ft 3in
    Height – 3.99m/13ft 1in
    Wing area – 23.92m^2/258sq ft
Weights: Empty – 2,667kg/5,880lb
    Maximum take-off – 3,674kg/8,100lb
Performance: Maximum speed – 550kph/342mph
    Service ceiling – 10,850m/35,600ft
    Range – 740km/460 miles
    Climb – 6,096m/20,000ft in 9 minutes, 6 seconds

ABOVE: **The He 59 was one of the easier wartime aircraft to identify thanks to its twin-float biplane open-cockpit arrangement.** RIGHT: **Rescue versions were accused of having a clandestine military role and were attacked by British aircraft.**

Heinkel He 59

Heinkel began to develop a 'reconnaissance-bomber' for the German military in 1930 but, like many other military aircraft under development in the country at the time, the project was presented to the world as a civil aircraft. When the second prototype (the He 59b) of the twin-engine He 59 biplane first flew in September 1931 it was a landplane with a conventional

ABOVE: **Powered by two 660hp engines, the He 59 was a large aircraft but had a range in excess of 1,600km/1,000 miles. Fuel was also carried in the aircraft's twin floats.**

undercarriage. Designed by Reinhold Mewes, it was the first prototype – the He 59a, which, confusingly, was second to fly in January 1942 – that tested a floatplane configuration. It was this version that became the basis for the production machines, 142 of which were built in three main variants.

Evaluation aircraft were designated He 59A (not to be confused with the He 59a) and were followed by a production version, the He 59B-1 armed with a machine-gun in the nose as well as the dorsal position. The He 59B-2 had an all-metal nose with a glazed bombing position and a ventral gun position. The B-3 was a reconnaissance machine while the C-1 was a trainer and the C-2 was a dedicated air-sea rescue aircraft equipped with inflatable dinghies and emergency supplies. The latter variant can be most readily identified by its fixed folding ladder and was used in the English Channel during the Battle of Britain.

The three-man He 59 was of mixed construction. The wings consisted of a wooden frame covered with fabric but with a plywood leading edge while the boxy fuselage was a primarily fabric-covered steel frame. The two floats also served as fuel tanks holding 900 litres/198 gallons each. In addition, an internal

fuselage tank and two extra fuel tanks could also be carried in the bomb bay.

The type saw action with the Condor Legion in the Spanish Civil War, and in the early stages of World War II the He 59 served as a torpedo and mine-laying aircraft. Some were used in a lightning raid operation and landed troops on a Dutch canal to seize a bridge.

The type was gradually relegated to training duties and all were retired by 1944.

The Finnish Air Force operated four of the aircraft for a period in 1943 to transport scouting troops behind enemy lines.

Heinkel He 59B-2

First flight: January 1932 (He 59a)
Power: Two 660hp BMW VI 6,0 ZU piston engines
Armament: Three 7.92mm machine-guns in nose, dorsal and ventral positions plus up to 1,000kg/2,205lb of bombs or a torpedo
Size: Wingspan – 23.7m/77ft 9in
Length – 17.4m/57ft 1in
Height – 7.1m/23ft 3.5in
Wing area – 153.3m²/1,650sq ft
Weights: Empty – 6215kg/13,702lb
Maximum take-off – 9,000kg/19,842lb
Performance: Maximum speed – 220kph/137mph
Ceiling – 3,500m/11,480ft
Range – 1,750km/1,087 miles
Climb – 225m/738ft per minute

LEFT: **Although this version, the He 60D, was armed with a forward-firing machine-gun, the aircraft was easy prey for fast and agile Allied fighters.**
ABOVE: **D-IXES was one of two prototypes of the He 60C – it was this version that served on all major German warships.**

Heinkel He 60

The single-engined Heinkel He 60 biplane floatplane was developed in 1932 as a reconnaissance aircraft to be carried and catapult launched from all large German warships. Designed by Heinkel engineer Reinhold Mewes, the designer of the He 59, the type was also used extensively by sea and coastal reconnaissance units well into World War II.

The prototype He 60a first flew in early 1933 but its original power plant proved inadequate. Upgrading of its engine did little to improve its performance but the He 60, ruggedly constructed to cope with catapult launches and rough seas, still entered service in 1933. Pilots praised the aircraft for its water-handling

The unarmed He 60A was the first version in Kriegsmarine (Navy) service, then the B model armed with a 7.9mm machine-gun in the observer's cockpit appeared but was soon succeeded by the improved He 60C, which entered service in 1934. The C model was operated from most German warships prior to World War II – the aircraft's multi-purpose floats contained spraying equipment that could either lay down a smoke screen or even spray mustard gas. Like so many

other German military aircraft, the type was evaluated during the Spanish Civil War and four examples remained in use in Spain until the end of World War II.

The type was relegated to training duties early in World War II but it continued to serve in the maritime reconnaissance role with shore-based units in the Mediterranean, North Sea, Crete and Greece despite its vulnerability to enemy fighters.

The aircraft was replaced in service first by the Heinkel He 114 and then by the Arado Ar 196 in service. All He 60s were phased out by October 1943.

LEFT: **Demonstrating its original purpose, an He 60 is pictured overflying the German Navy's light cruiser *Köln*. The type extended the ship's view well beyond the sea-level horizon. It served in the shore-based role with the Kriegsmarine until late 1943.**

Heinkel He 60B

First flight: 1933
Power: One 660hp BMW VI 12-cylinder
    piston engine
Armament: One 7.9mm machine-gun in
    rear cockpit
Size: Wingspan – 13.5m/44ft 3.5in
    Length – 11.5m/37ft 8.75in
    Height – 5.3m/17ft 4.5in
    Wing area – 56.2m²/604sq ft
Weights: Empty – 2,725kg/6,009lb
    Maximum take-off – 3,425kg/7,552lb
Performance: Maximum speed – 240kph/149mph
    Ceiling – 5,000m/16,405ft
    Range – 950km/590 miles
    Climb – 1,000m/3,280ft in 3 minutes, 12 seconds

LEFT: **Although World War II was the swansong for twin-float seaplane types, a number of military aircraft, including the He 115, played a significant role in the conflict.**
ABOVE: **With the ability to carry 1,250kg/ 2,756lb of ordnance, the aircraft had real destructive capability.**

Heinkel He 115

The largest and most powerful production twin-float seaplane used in World War II, the He 115 was developed in the mid-1930s as a torpedo-bomber, mine-laying and reconnaissance aircraft to replace the company's earlier He 59. Despite the fact that the He 115 was in many ways obsolete at the start of World War II, the type continued in Luftwaffe service almost to the end of the conflict. This was due to the fact that while carrying out its main duty of mine-laying at night, it was able to operate with little interference from Allied aircraft or defences.

The type had a crew of three with the pilot housed in a cockpit over the wing's leading edge. The observer's position was in the glazed nose while the radio operator sat in a separate cockpit positioned over the trailing edge. Defensive armament initially consisted of one forward-firing and one rear-firing 7.9mm machine-gun operated by the observer and

ABOVE: **At the outbreak of World War II the Luftwaffe had eight He 115s in front-line service on coastal-patrol duties. During the invasion of Norway, German forces were attacked by exported He 115s serving in the Norwegian Naval Air Service.**

radio operator respectively. In early versions the bomb bay (located in the fuselage beneath the wing) could carry one 800kg/1,763lb torpedo or three 250kg/550lb bombs.

The He 115 V1 (civil serial D-AEHF) prototype made its first flight in 1936 and this robust and reliable aircraft impressed the Luftwaffe sufficiently that 115 were ordered for the air force's *Seeflieger*. In March 1938, after some modifications including a much-streamlined nose, this aircraft set eight speed records over 1,000km/621-mile and 2,000km/1,243-mile courses, carrying payloads up to 2,000kg/4,409lb.

By the third prototype (the He 115 V3), the design had been refined and was very similar to the production versions with the pilot and radio operator cockpits covered and joined by one large 'greenhouse'-type canopy. Production versions also featured a dual-control facility where the essential flying controls were duplicated in the rear cockpit. This would have enabled the radio operator to land the aircraft if the pilot was indisposed. The first production version, the He 115A-1 also featured an underwing bomb rack for two 250kg/550lb bombs.

The He 115 caught the eye of the Swedish and the Norwegians who both placed export orders for the type. Six went to Norway while twelve were ordered for Sweden.

At the start of World War II, 'naval co-operation' unit 1./*Küstenfliegerstaffel* 106 became the first unit to receive the type. Following the completion of the 62nd aircraft in early 1940, the production line at Heinkel's Marienhe plant closed with manufacturing shifting to Einswarden.

The He 115B-1 introduced increased fuel capacity and therefore significantly increased range – up to 3,350km/ 2,080 miles compared to the 2,000km/1,242 miles of the A-series. Large 1,000kg/2,200lb parachute mines could be carried by some B-1s though clearly over a reduced range due to the considerable weight increase.

LEFT: **The He 115 could carry a devastating 500kg/1,102lb torpedo, and proved to be a most effective anti-shipping weapon. On July 2, 1942, eight of these twin-float seaplanes attacked Allied convoy PQ 17, and two days later an He 115 torpedoed and severely damaged the US freighter *Christopher Newport*. Note the extensive nose glazing.**

The type was used by coastal reconnaissance units of the Luftwaffe and when war broke out dropped parachute mines in British waters. The first such mission on the night of November 20–21, 1939, saw aircraft of 3./*Küstenfliegerstaffel* 906 drop mines off the Essex coast and at the mouth of the Thames.

During the 1940 German invasion of Norway, Norwegian Naval Air Service He 115s (and two captured German machines) were put into action against German forces. Some were subsequently flown to the UK where they were modified and, sometimes sporting German markings, used for clandestine operations. One bright sunny day, one of these landed in Tripoli harbour where it picked up two British agents before flying back to its Malta base, completely unmolested by the Luftwaffe.

The type's success as a mine-layer led to a reopening of production in late 1943 resulting in a total production run of around 500.

ABOVE: **An excellent view of the He 115's large wing area and that of the tail. This is an He 155B taxiing as the radio operator converses with the navigator.**
LEFT: **Notice the large glazed nose on the aircraft, which gave the navigator excellent all-round vision. The sheer size of the aircraft is evident as the crew arms and prepares the aircraft for its next flight while the aircraft's captain looks on.**

Heinkel He 115B-1

First flight: 1936 (prototype)
Power: Two BMW 856hp 132N 9-cylinder radial piston engines
Armament: One fixed forward-firing and one rear-firing 7.9mm machine-guns plus up to 1,250kg/2,756lb of torpedoes, mines or bombs
Size: Wingspan – 22m/72ft 2in
    Length – 17.3m/56ft 9in
    Height – 6.6m/21ft 8in
    Wing area – 86.7m²/933sq ft
Weights: Empty – 5,300kg/11,684lb
    Maximum take-off – 10,400kg/22,928lb
Performance: Maximum speed – 353kph/220mph
    Service ceiling – 5,500m/18,005ft
    Range – 3,350km/2,080 miles
    Climb – 235m/770ft per minute

LEFT: **Although the early E7K was virtually obsolete by the start of World War II, many of the machines that survived ended up as kamikaze machines.**
ABOVE: **The E7K was a comparatively large single-engined biplane. With a crew of three the aircraft had an unfortunate reputation for engine unreliability.**

Kawanishi E7K

The Kawanishi E7K was a Japanese three-seat reconnaissance floatplane that was to be given the wartime Allied codename of 'Alf'. The E7K resulted from a 1932 Imperial Japanese Navy (IJN) requirement, which asked the Kawanishi Aircraft Company to produce a replacement for the company's Kawanishi E5K reconnaissance seaplane for IJN service. The proposed replacement, designated the Kawanishi E7K1, was a conventional equal-span biplane powered by a 620hp Hiro 91 engine.

The prototype flew for the first time on February 6, 1933, and after evaluation and competitive trials against an Aichi machine, the type was chosen for production as the Navy Type 94 Reconnaissance Seaplane. The aircraft

could operate from ships or from land bases and was equally adept on anti-submarine patrols and reconnaissance missions. The E7K entered service in early 1935 and though generally liked by its crews, its engine was considered unreliable.

Kawanishi tried an improved Hiro 91 engine but reliability was still an issue. The company later proposed the E7K2 powered by a Mitsubishi Zuisei 11 radial engine and this version had its first flight in August 1938. The IJN were sufficiently impressed by the improved version that they ordered production aircraft under the designation Navy Type 94 Reconnaissance Seaplane Model 2. The E7K1 was meanwhile retrospectively redesignated Navy Type 94 Reconnaissance Seaplane Model 1.

Both versions were in use at the start of the war in the Pacific although the E7K1 was soon removed from front-line duties to assume training and utility roles. The EK72 remained in front-line use until 1943.

Towards the end of the Pacific war, all available examples of both versions were stripped and converted for use on kamikaze missions.

Production consisted of 183 examples of the E7K1 of which 57 were subcontracted to Nippon. A total of 350 of the improved E7K2s were built, with 60 built by subcontractor Nippon.

LEFT: **The Kawanishi E7K, or 'Alf', was able to stay aloft for almost 12 hours – a great performance for a shipborne reconnaissance type, and one that enabled the aircraft to cover great areas of ocean in search of enemy craft.**

Kawanishi E7K2

First flight: February 6, 1933 (prototype)
Power: Mitsubishi 870hp Zuisei 11 radial engine
Armament: One forward-firing 7.7mm machine-gun, one flexible 7.7mm machine-gun in each of the rear cockpits and one downwards-firing ventral position plus up to 120kg/264lb of bombs
Size: Wingspan – 14m/45ft 11in
Length – 10.5m/34ft 5in
Height – 4.85m/15ft 11in
Wing area – 43.6m²/469sq ft
Weights: Empty – 2,100kg/4,630lb
Maximum take-off – 3,300kg/7,275lb
Performance: Maximum speed – 275kph/171mph
Ceiling – 7,060m/2,3165ft
Range – 1,845km/1,147 miles
Climb – 3,000m/9,840ft in 9 minutes, 6 seconds

Kawanishi H6K

The Kawanishi H6K was a large Imperial Japanese Navy maritime patrol flying boat with its origins in a 1933 IJN requirement for a high-performance flying boat that could cruise at 220kph/137mph and have a range of 4,500km/2,795 miles.

The four-engined aircraft had a high parasol-type wing with a slight dihedral and was braced by struts connected to the fuselage. The aircraft's distinctive wings had parallel leading and trailing edges for half their length and then tapered at the point where the wing-mounted floats were fitted. The aircraft's shallow hull was all-metal and was modified for better on-water performance following the prototype's first flight in July 1936. The four 840hp Nakajima Hikari radial engines fitted to the prototype did not provide enough power but with more powerful engines,

the Type 97 Large Flying Boat was cleared to enter service in 1938 becoming the Navy's only long-range maritime reconnaissance flying boat in service at the time.

The type first saw action during the Sino-Japanese War and most of the 217 built were used during the Pacific War during which it was codenamed 'Mavis' by the Allies. Its range and endurance (it could fly on 24-hour patrols) made it a key aircraft in the Japanese military inventory – it even undertook long-range bombing missions on targets such as Rabaul.

As the Allies deployed more modern fighters in the Pacific, they started to take their toll on the large slow flying boat so the H6Ks came to be limited to

operations in areas where Allied fighter presence was limited.

The Overseas (Ocean) Division of Japan Air Lines operated 18 examples of the H6K2-L unarmed 18-passenger transport version on Central and Western Pacific routes.

It was Kawanishi's own H8K that replaced the H6K in military service after which the surviving H6Ks were converted for troop carrying. Some H6K2-Ls based in the Netherlands East Indies were seized by Indonesian nationalists and were operated post-war for a time.

Kawanishi H6K4

First flight: July 14, 1936 (prototype)

Power: Four Mitsubishi 1,070hp Kinsei 43 engines

Armament: Total of five 7.7mm machine-guns in open bow, forward turret, side blisters and open dorsal positions, one 20mm cannon in tail turret and up to 800kg/1,764lb of bombs

Size: Wingspan – 40m/131ft 2in
Length – 25.63m/84ft 1in
Height – 6.27m/20ft 7in
Wing area – 170m²/1,830sq ft

Weights: Empty – 11,707kg/25,810lb
Maximum take-off – 21,500kg/47,399lb

Performance: Maximum speed – 340kph/211mph
Ceiling – 9,610m/31,530ft
Range – 6,080km/3,779 miles
Climb – 5,000m/16,400ft in 13 minutes, 31 seconds

ABOVE: Some versions of the Kawanishi H6K were unarmed and were used for transport and communication duties – these were easy targets for Allied aircraft and a number fell to enemy guns.

Kawanishi H8K

The H8K was developed in response to a 1938 Japanese Navy specification for a replacement for its then new H6K, the service's standard maritime patrol flying boat. The new design was to have a 30 per cent higher speed and 50 per cent greater range than the H6K. The requirement also called for a long-range aircraft with better performance than Britain's Short Sunderland or the American Sikorsky XPBS-1. The designers produced one of the finest military flying boats ever built and certainly the fastest and best of World War II.

To give the aircraft the required range, the wings contained eight small, unprotected fuel tanks and a further six large tanks in the fuselage or, more correctly, hull. The hull tanks were partially self-sealing and also boasted a carbon dioxide fire extinguisher system. Ingeniously, the tanks were placed so that if any leaked the fuel would collect in a fuel 'bilge' and then be pumped to an undamaged tank. The aircraft was a flying fuel tank with 15,816 litres/3,479 gallons being a typical fuel load

TOP: **The H8K2-L transport version of this very capable flying boat was modified to carry passengers on an additional upper deck.**

ABOVE: **The H8K was a truly great flying boat that was far from an easy target for enemy fighters thanks to its impressive armament. Nevertheless, on the ground or on water, the large aircraft was easy prey when attacked from the air.**

and accounting for some 29 per cent of the take-off weight. The aircraft positively bristled with defensive armament – a 20mm cannon was carried in each of the powered nose, dorsal and tail turrets with two more in opposite beam blisters. A further three 7.7mm machine-guns were in port and starboard beam hatches and in the ventral position. The crew positions

ABOVE: **This example of an 'Emily' was captured at the end of the war and evaluated by the victors. The Allies were intrigued by the 'Emily', acknowledged as the best flying boat of its class in service at the time, and were keen to learn from the large Kawanishi boat.**

were well armoured – this all ensured that Allied fighter pilots treated the Japanese 'boat' with considerable respect as it was far from an easy 'kill'. It was the most heavily defended flying boat of World War II and one which Allied fighter pilots found hard to down in aerial combat.

The Navy were appropriately impressed with the aircraft, but flight testing of the H8K in late 1940 was far from uneventful and numerous features of the aircraft had to be revised – the heavy aircraft's narrow hull, for example, caused uncontrollable porpoising in the water. When the nose lifted from the water's surface, the whole aircraft became unstable. The design team revised the hull and production of the H8K1 (Navy Type 2 Flying Boat Model 11) began in mid-1941. Total production was a mere 175 aircraft produced in the H8K1, H8K2 (improved engines, heavier armament and radar) and 3H8K2-L (transport) versions.

The H8K was powered by four 1,530hp Kasei 11s or 12s – the latter bestowed better high-altitude performance and powered late-production H8K1s. The aircraft's offensive load, carried under the inner wing, was either two 801kg/1,764lb. torpedoes, eight 250kg/551lb bombs, or sixteen 60kg/132lb. bombs or depth charges.

The H8K made its combat debut on the night of March 4–5, 1942. The night bombing raid on the island of Oahu, Hawaii, was over so great a distance that even the long-range H8K had to put down to refuel from a submarine en route. Although due to bad weather the target was not bombed, the raid showed that the H8K was a formidable weapon of war.

The H8K's deep hull lent itself to the development of a transport version, the H8K2-L with two passenger decks. The lower deck reached from the nose to some two-thirds of the way along the fuselage while the upper deck extended from the wing to the back of the hull. Seats or benches could accommodate from 29 passengers or 64 troops in appropriately differing levels of comfort. Armament was reduced as was fuel-carrying capability with the removal of hull tanks.

ABOVE: **From being dangerously unstable in testing, the H8K went on to be among the best military flying boats ever produced.** BELOW: **The comparatively fast H8K first flew into action in March 1942. Later versions of the H8K2 (the most numerous production model) were fitted with ASV radar that greatly enhanced their capability and threat status to Allied shipping.**

ABOVE: **Of the 175 aircraft produced, only 4 examples survived after the end of World War II. One was this H8K2 that was captured by US forces at the end of hostilities and taken to the US for evaluation. It was returned to Japan in 1979 and was displayed in Tokyo until 2004, but is now preserved at Kanoya Naval Air Base Museum in Japan. It is a rare example of one of the best military flying boats.**

Kawanishi H8K2

First flight: Late 1940
Power: Four Mitsubishi 1,850hp Kasei radial engines
Armament: 20mm cannon in bow, dorsal and tail turrets and in beam blisters plus four 7.7mm machine-guns in cockpit, ventral and side hatches
Size: Wingspan – 38m/124ft 8in
Length – 28.13m/92ft 4in
Height – 9.15m/30ft
Wing area – 160m²/1,722sq ft
Weights: Empty – 18,380kg/40,521lb
Maximum take-off – 32,500kg/71,650lb
Performance: Maximum speed – 467kph/290mph
Service ceiling – 8,760m/28,740ft
Range – 7,180km/4460 miles
Climb – 480m/1,575ft per minute

LEFT: **The original N1K1 floatplane fighter was designed for a very specific purpose, but the need for the aircraft passed as the war turned in the Allies' favour. This led to the ungainly looking arrangement being separated, and the N1K1-S was born. Note the very large central float and stabilizing outer floats.**

Kawanishi N1K1-/K2-J

Land-based aircraft have often been turned into floatplanes, but in the case of the Kawanishi N1K1-J *Shiden* (violet lightning) it was, uniquely, a landplane derived from a floatplane fighter. Kawanishi's earlier N1K1 *Kyofu* (strong or mighty wind) was an Imperial Japanese Navy floatplane fighter built to support forward offensive operations in areas where airstrips were not available. However, by the time the aircraft entered service in 1943, Japan was on the defensive and had little use for the N1K1. Codenamed 'Rex' by the Allies, it was no match for US Navy carrier fighters due to the large heavy float it carried.

Two years earlier, Kawanishi engineers had proposed a land-based version without a float and a prototype was produced by Kawanishi as a speculative private venture aircraft. This flew on December 27, 1942, powered by a Nakajima Homare radial engine that replaced the less-powerful Mitsubishi Kasei used

in the N1K1. The aircraft retained the mid-mounted wing of the floatplane version, and this and the large propeller called for long landing gear. The undercarriage proved to be problematic as, due to poor heat-treating, the landing gear would often simply rip off as the aircraft touched down. More were reportedly lost to this fault than to Allied action.

The new version was designated Kawanishi N1K1-J *Shiden*. Codenamed 'George' by the Allies, this Japanese fighter entered service during the last year of World War II, appearing throughout the Pacific from May 1944. It possessed heavy armament and, unusually for a Japanese fighter, could absorb considerable battle damage. In spite of production problems and shortages of parts caused by B-29 raids on the Japanese homeland, over 1,400 were built and were formidable foes. Unique automatic combat flaps that increased lift during

LEFT: **The Kawanishi N1K2-J was an oustanding combat aircraft – note the low wing, the position of which changed for this version. Had the aircraft appeared earlier and in great numbers, it would have caused the Allies great losses.**

LEFT: **Two N1K1s prepare for flight. It was rare for an effective land-based fighter to be derived from a floatplane design.** ABOVE: **The United States captured and evaluated a number of examples of the type – here US service personnel assess a captured aircraft.**

extreme combat activity dramatically enhanced manoeuvrability. The 'George' proved to be one of the best all-round fighters in the Pacific theatre but it lacked the high-altitude performance needed to counter the devastating B-29 raids. The N1K1-J evenly matched the F6F Hellcat and could win fights with Allied aircraft such as the F4U Corsair and P-51 Mustang. Despite such ability, it was produced too late and in too few numbers to affect the outcome of the war.

Early versions had poor visibility due to the mid-mounted wing and inadequate landing gear and so the N1K2-J version known as the *Shiden-Kai*, 'George 21' to the Allies, was produced. The main difference was the moving of the wing from mid to low position that reduced the need for the troublesome long landing gear. The prototype of this variant first flew in December 1943, and was soon adopted as the standard Japanese land-based fighter and fighter-bomber. The N1K2-J could be built in half the time of the earlier version and

became a truly outstanding fighter aircraft that could hold its own against the best of the Allied fighters. The Homare engine was retained as there was really no alternative even though reliability remained a major problem.

Nevertheless, the *Shiden-Kai* proved to be one of the best fighters operating in the Pacific theatre – it had a roll rate of 82 degrees per second at 386kph/240mph. It was, however, less successful as a bomber interceptor due to its poor rate of climb and poor high-altitude engine performance. Allied bombing raids disrupted production so that only 415 examples were completed.

Total production of all versions reached 1,435, and three aircraft are known to survive in US aviation museums. One is at the National Museum of Naval Aviation at Pensacola, Florida; a second is at the United States Air Force Museum at Wright-Patterson Air Force Base near Dayton, Ohio, while the third is preserved by the National Air and Space Museum.

ABOVE: **Although the type entered service in 1943, the Allies were already well aware of the type, and had even assigned it the codename 'Rex', due to the capture of Japanese documents that spoke of the aircraft and its planned uses. Of the 1,435 built, only 3 survive.**

Kawanishi N1K2-J ●

First flight: December 31, 1943
Power: Nakajima 1990hp NK9H Homare 21 radial piston engine
Armament: Four 20mm cannon in wings plus two 250kg/551lb bombs under wings
Size: Span – 12m/39ft 4.5in
  Length – 9.35m/30ft 8in
  Height – 3.96m/13ft
  Wing area – 23.5m²/253sq ft
Weights: Empty – 2,657kg/5,858lb
  Maximum take-off – 4,860kg/10,714lb
Performance: Maximum speed – 595kph/370mph
  Ceiling – 10,760m/35,300ft
  Range – 2,335km/1,451 miles with drop tanks
  Climb – 1,000m/3,280ft per minute

Martin Mariner

With its history of producing flying boats, Martin began work on a design in 1937 to replace the Consolidated Catalina in US Navy service. Martin's Model 162, naval designation XPBM-1 (Experimental Patrol Bomber Martin 1) had a flat twin-fin tail, inward-retracting wing-floats, a deep hull and shoulder-mounted gull wings. The gull-wing design was used to produce the greatest possible distance between the engines and the surface of the sea water from which the aircraft would operate. An approximately half-scale single-seat version of the design was produced to test the aerodynamics –

ABOVE: **A US Navy PBM-3. Production of this version required the building of a new factory complex. The -3 was powered by improved Pratt & Whitney R-2600-12 engines. Note the flying boat's hull shape.** BELOW LEFT: **A US Navy PBM starts its engine at a Caribbean naval air station as ground crew stand by with a fire extinguisher. Note the large radome aft of the cockpit. The aircraft's all-metal two-step hull can also be seen in this view.**

its success led to the first flight of the full-scale prototype XPBM-1 in February 1939.

The results of test flights called for a redesign of the tail which resulted in the dihedral configuration that matched the angle of the main wings. The aircraft had been ordered before the test flight so the first production model, the PBM-1, appeared quite quickly in October 1940 with service deliveries being complete by April 1941 – impressive even for the uncertain days before the US entered World War II. By now the type was named Mariner, had a crew of seven and was armed with five 0.50in Browning machine-guns. One gun was mounted in a flexible position in the tail, one in a flexible-mount on each side of the rear fuselage; another was fitted in a rear dorsal turret while one was deployed in a nose turret. In addition, the PBM-1 could carry up to 900kg/1,985lb of bombs or depth charges in bomb bays that were, unusually, fitted in the engine nacelles. The doors of the bomb bays looked like those of landing gear but the Mariner did not have amphibian capability at this stage in its development.

In late 1940, the US Navy ordered 379 improved Model 162Bs or PBM-3s although around twice that number were actually produced. This order alone required the US Government-aided construction of a new Martin plant in

Maryland. The -3 differed from the -1 mainly by the installation of uprated Pratt & Whitney 1,700hp R-2600-12 engines, larger fixed wing floats and larger bomb bays housed in enlarged nacelles. This version also featured powered nose and dorsal turrets. Early PBM-3s had three-bladed propellers but production versions soon included four-bladed propellers.

The PBM-3C rolled out in late 1942 as the next major version with 274 built. It had better armour protection for the crew, twin-gun front and dorsal turrets, an improved tail turret still with a single gun, and Air-to-Surface-Vessel radar. In addition, many PBM-3Cs were fitted with an underwing searchlight in the field to assist with the finding of enemy craft at night.

US Navy Mariners saw extensive use in the Pacific, guarding the Atlantic western approaches and in defence of the Panama Canal. It was felt that as most Mariners were not likely to encounter fighter opposition, much of the defensive armament could be deleted – once the guns, turrets and ammunition were removed, the weight saving resulted in a 25 per cent increase in the range of the lighter PBM-3S anti-submarine version. The nose guns were, however, retained for offensive fire against U-boats and other surface targets. Despite this development, a more heavily armed and armoured version, the PBM-3D, was produced by re-engining some 3Cs. Larger non-retractable floats and self-sealing fuel tanks were also a feature of this version.

Deliveries of the more powerfully engined PBM-5 began in August 1944, with 589 delivered before production ceased at the end of the war. With the PBM-5A amphibian version, of which 40 were built, the Mariner finally acquired a tricycle landing gear. The Mariner continued to serve with the US Navy and US Coast Guard (USCG) into the early 1950s and over 500 were still in service at the time of the Korean War. The USCG retired its last Mariner in 1958.

During World War II, 25 PBM-3Bs, designated Mariner G.R.1, were allocated to the RAF under Lend-Lease arrangements. In late 1943, the type was operated for seven weeks from a base in Scotland but never entered front-line RAF service.

ABOVE: **The Mariner had a range in excess of 322km/200 miles and features included a galley, sleeping quarters, sound proofing, heating and a form of air conditioning too. Note the vast radome atop the aircraft.**

BELOW: **A Mariner could land to take surrender of an enemy submarine, having attacked it from the air. The type was developed throughout its production.**

ABOVE: **The Mariner's high wing, with its entire hinged trailing edge, and the aircraft's distinctive dihedral twin-fin tail makes the Martin flying boat very easy to identify.**

Martin PBM-3D Mariner

First flight: February 18, 1939 (XPBM-1)
Power: Two Wright 1,900hp R-2600-22 Cyclone radial piston engines
Armament: Eight 0.5in machine-guns in nose 3,628kg/8,000lb of bombs or depth charges
Size: Wingspan – 35.97m/118ft
   Length – 24.33m/79ft 10in
   Height – 8.38m/27ft 6in
   Wing area – 130.8m²/1,408sq ft
Weights: Empty – 15,048kg/33,175lb
   Maximum take-off – 26,308kg/58,000lb
Performance: Maximum speed – 340kph/211mph
   Service ceiling – 6,035m/19,800ft
   Range – 3,605km/2,240 miles
   Climb – 244m/800ft per minute

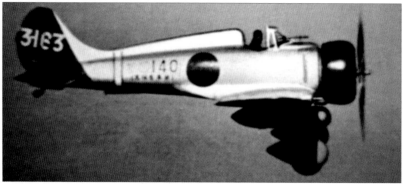

Mitsubishi A5M

The 350kph/217mph top speed specified in a 1934 Imperial Japanese Navy fighter specification seemed to be a tall order at the time. To ease the designers' burden, the need to operate the new fighter from aircraft carriers was not even written into the specification. However, Mitsubishi's offering, the Ka-14, which was first flown in February 1935, showed a top speed of 450kph/280mph that far exceeded the specified speed required.

It was designed with minimum drag in mind – the fuselage had a small cross section, the aluminium skin was flush riveted and the fixed undercarriage had streamlined spats. It was perhaps too complex a design and the inverted gull-wing that caused some handling headaches was replaced with a more conventional low wing. With this change and powered by a 585hp Kotobuki 2-KAI-1 engine, the type was ordered into production as the Navy Type 96 Carrier Fighter Model 1 (Mitsubishi A5M1).

The A5M was the world's first monoplane shipboard fighter and was the direct ancestor of Mitsubishi's later Zero. The type began to enter service in early 1937 and was soon in action in the Sino-Japanese War.

The subsequent A5M2a (basically the same aircraft powered by a 610hp KAI-3) and A5M2b (with the 640hp Kotobuki 3 engine) became the most important Navy fighters during Japan's war with China. Until the A5M2a arrival in theatre, the Japanese were suffering heavy losses but after only a short time the A5M2a achieved total air superiority. Experience of air operations in China speeded up development of the A5M2b with a three-bladed propeller driven by the more powerful engine and the luxury of an enclosed cockpit under a greenhouse-style canopy that in fact proved unpopular with pilots and was omitted on late-build A5M2bs. All had a fixed non-retractable undercarriage with wheel spats for improved aerodynamics. The A5M2s were so effective in China that all Chinese air units were withdrawn out of range of the Japanese fighters.

The final, best known and most numerous production version was the A5M4 that was developed in response to the Chinese withdrawal – greater range was the most important consideration. The A5M4 looked identical to the late production open-cockpit A5M2bs but was powered by the

710hp Nakajima Kotobuki 41 and carried a 160-litre/ 35.2-gallon drop tank. It entered service in China in 1938 and with its longer range greatly extended the area of Japanese air superiority while driving the less able Chinese air units even further away from the battle area.

As some A5Ms were still in service at the beginning of World War II, United States intelligence sources believed the A5M was Japan's primary Navy fighter, when in fact Mitsubishi's much more capable Zero had all but replaced the 'Claudes' on first-line aircraft carriers. It was soon withdrawn for second-line duties (including advanced fighter training) as it was no match for the newer Allied fighters. A dedicated trainer version with twin cockpits, the A5M4-K, was also built – 103 were produced – and continued in use for fighter training long after the regular A5M left front-line service.

As the war in the Pacific approached its desperate end, remaining A5M4s were used in kamikaze attacks against Allied ships off the Japanese coast. Total A5M production numbered 1,094.

TOP: The 'Claude' was the Japanese Navy's first monoplane fighter and at the start of the war in the Pacific equipped three wings on Japanese light carriers.

ABOVE: The Imperial Japanese Navy were early adopters of droppable auxiliary fuel tanks as a means of increasing their aircraft's range. This policy gave the Japanese an early advantage when war broke out in the Pacific.

BELOW: The A5M4 was designed in response to a need for increased range to enable its pilots to take the battle to Chinese pilots who were withdrawn beyond the range of earlier versions. Note the guns just forward of the cockpit.

Mitsubishi A5M4

First flight: February 4, 1935
Power: Nakajima 710hp Kotobuki 41 (Bristol Jupiter) 9-cylinder radial piston engine
Armament: Two 7.7mm machine-guns firing on each side of upper cylinder of engine plus two racks for two 30kg/66lb bombs under outer wings
Size: Wingspan – 11m/36ft 1in
Length – 7.55m/24ft 9.25in
Height – 3.2m/10ft 6in
Wing area – 17.8m²/192sq ft
Weights: Empty – 1,216kg/2,681lb
Maximum take-off – 1,707kg/3,763lb
Performance: Maximum speed – 440kph/273mph
Ceiling – 10,000m/32,800ft
Range – 1,200km/746 miles
Climb – 850m/2,790ft per minute

Mitsubishi A6M Zero-Sen

The Zero is rightly Japan's most famous wartime aircraft and was perhaps most significantly the first shipboard fighter capable of beating its land-based opponents. It had its origins in a 1937 Japanese Navy requirement for a new fighter with a maximum speed exceeding 500kph/310mph to replace Mitsubishi's A5M carrier fighter. The new aircraft had to climb to 3,000m/9,840ft in 3.5 minutes, exhibit manoeuvrability and have range exceeding any existing fighter, and carry the impressive armament of two cannon and two machine-guns. Only Mitsubishi accepted the challenge and design work began under the direction of Jiro Horikoshi.

The prototype was completed on March 16, 1939, first flew on April 1 and was accepted by the Navy on September 14, 1939, as the A6M1 Carrier Fighter. The chosen powerplant was the lightweight Mitsubishi Zuisei, later replaced by the more powerful Nakajima *Sakae* (Prosperity) 925hp radial which was only slightly larger and heavier than the original *Zuisei*. With its

ABOVE: **The Mitsubishi Zero, with its high performance, obsessed the US military, who were keen to understand the enemy aircraft. This example in US markings was assembled in the USA in December 1942 from five captured aircraft.**

new-found power, the fighter amply exceeded the original performance requirements which had been regarded as impossible a few months earlier. At this time, production models of Navy aircraft were assigned type numbers based on the last number of the Japanese year in which production began, and as 1940 was the year 2600 in the Japanese calendar, the A6M series was known as the Zero-Sen (Type 00 fighter).

Even before the final acceptance of the A6M2 as a production fighter, the Japanese Navy requested that a number of machines be delivered for operational use in China to meet growing aerial resistance. Accordingly, 15 A6M2s were delivered for service in China and first appeared over

ABOVE: **Having achieved a high level of success during the war with China, the Zero accounted for over 60 per cent of the Japanese Navy's carrier-borne fighter. It was the first carrier fighter to meet land-based fighters on equal performance terms.**

LEFT: **The Zero epitomized Japanese wartime air power.** ABOVE: **The RAF also evaluated captured Zeros. These aircraft, pictured in 1946, were flown by Japanese pilots under RAF supervision.**

Chungking in August 1940 when the Zeros shot down all the defending Chinese fighters. Washington was informed about the new high-performance Japanese fighter but no heed was taken and so its appearance over Pearl Harbor came as a complete surprise to the American forces. Its subsequent appearance in every major battle area in the opening days of the war seemed to indicate that Japan possessed almost unlimited supplies of the high-performance fighter. In fact, in December 1941, the Japanese Navy had well over 400 Zero fighters. In 1941–42 the Zero certainly got the better of all opposing fighters whether it flew from carriers or had to operate over long distances from land bases. During a Japanese carrier-raid on Ceylon, Zeros easily out-turned opposing RAF Hawker Hurricanes, aircraft that until then had been regarded as outstandingly manoeuvrable.

In mid-1942 the Allies eventually acquired an intact specimen and found that the Zero possessed many shortcomings. It was shipped back to the USA where exhaustive tests revealed the fighter's faults and shattered the myths that surrounded it. The tables were turned at the Battle

of Midway in June 1942 when the A6M5 version came up against a new generation of US Navy and Army fighters, with powerful engines and heavy protection for their pilot and fuel tanks. Against them the Zero, still basically the design which had flown first in April 1939, offered minimal protection for pilot and fuel tanks and from 1943 the Zeros fell like flies. The installation of the 1,560hp Kinsei engine brought the A6M8, the ultimate Zero, closer to the performance of Allied fighters but it was too late. The value of the fighter declined steadily and its lowest point was reached when it was selected as the first aircraft to be used intentionally as suicide attack (kamikaze or divine-wind) aircraft. The outstanding success of this form of attack led to the formation of dedicated kamikaze units, and the bomb-carrying Zeros became the prime suicide attack bombers of the Navy.

More Zero-Sens were produced than any other wartime Japanese aircraft. Mitsubishi alone produced 3,879 aircraft, Nakajima built 6,215 which, together with the 844 trainer and floatplane variants produced by Sasebo, Hitachi and Nakajima, brought the grand total of A6M series aircraft to 10,938.

ABOVE: **This Mitsubishi A6M3 was one of a number taken to the US and thoroughly tested. This aircraft is pictured over the United States on July 1, 1944.**

Mitsubishi A6M5 Zero

First flight: August, 1943
Power: Nakajima 1130hp NK1C Sakae 21 14-cylinder two-row radial piston engine
Armament: Two 20mm cannon in wing, two 7.7mm machine-guns in fuselage, plus two 60kg/132lb on underwing racks
Size: Wingspan – 11m/36ft 1in
Length – 9.06m/29ft 9in
Height – 2.98m/9ft 8in
Wing area – 21.3m²/229sq ft
Weights: Empty – 1,876kg/4,136lb
Maximum take-off – 2,733kg/6,025lb
Performance: Maximum speed – 570kph/354mph
Ceiling – 11,500m/37,730ft
Range – 1,920km/1,200 miles with drop tanks
Climb – 6,000m/19,685ft in 7 minutes, 3 seconds

Nakajima B5N

The Nakajima B5N was designed by a team led by Katsuji Nakamura to a 1935 Imperial Japanese Navy (IJN) requirement for a Yokosuka B4Y replacement. The Nakajima B5N was the IJN's only shipborne torpedo-bomber at the start of the Pacific War, and at that point it was the best carrier-borne torpedo-bomber in the world. Although as the war progressed it was considered obsolete compared to Allied counterparts, the B5N served until the end of World War II.

Internally designated Type K by Nakajima, it successfully competed with the Mitsubishi B5M for a production contract. This low-wing monoplane with its crew of three – pilot, navigator/bombardier/observer, and radio operator/gunner – and powered by a Nakajima Hikan radial engine, first flew in January 1937. Within a year, production versions, now with the full designation Type 97 Carrier Attack Bomber, were operating from Japan's carriers while shore-based units were deployed in China.

Combat experience in the Sino-Japanese War revealed weaknesses in the B5N1, specifically the lack of protection offered to the crew and the aircraft's fuel tanks. The Navy were unwilling to compromise the type's performance by the addition of armour and more defensive guns. Instead, Nakajima sought to improve the aircraft's performance through

ABOVE: **A B5N2. The B5N1 was supposedly refined and improved following combat experience of the type in the war with China, but in reality the later models' performance was little different.** BELOW: **Despite its shortcomings, in 1941 the B5N torpedo-bomber was among the best in the world and went on to inflict great losses on the Allies.**

streamlining and the installation of a more powerful engine which together would hopefully enable the aircraft to outrun enemy fighters. This new version, the B5N2, was in service by 1939 having the more powerful Sakae 11 engine covered with a smaller cowling. Armament and bomb load were unchanged compared to the earlier version (now known as the B5N1), and the B5N2 remained in production until 1943. Performance was only marginally improved compared to the earlier version.

At the time of the Japanese attack on Pearl Harbor in December 1941, the B5N2 had fully replaced the B5N1 with front-line torpedo-bomber units. There were 144 B5Ns (both 1s and 2s) involved in the Pearl Harbor attack, and in the year that followed, the type sank the US carriers *Lexington* at Coral Sea, *Yorktown* at Midway, and *Hornet* at the Battle of Santa Cruz in October 1942.

Allocated the reporting name 'Kate' by the Allies, the B5N was a serious threat – but when carrying a full load, its poor

defensive armament of just one machine-gun made it an easy target for Allied fighters. As the Allies gained control of the skies over the Pacific and the B5N2 fleet began to suffer heavy losses, the type was gradually withdrawn as a torpedo-bomber.

Having excellent range, the 'Kate' was then assigned to anti-submarine (some with early radars and magnetic anomaly detectors) and maritime reconnaissance duties in areas beyond the range of Allied fighters. Others were used for training and target-towing while some B5Ns were used as conventional bombers during the unsuccessful defence of the Philippines in October 1944. The B5N also became the basis for the Nakajima B6N Tenzan which eventually replaced it in front-line service with the Japanese Navy.

When production ceased in 1943 a total of 1,149 had been built – Nakajima completed 669, subcontractor Aichi made 200 and the Navy's Hiro Air Arsenal built 280. Of the many produced, no complete examples survive. A partial airframe recovered from Russia may be restored and rebuilt, but until then the replicas based on North American Harvard/Texans made for the 1970 film *Tora! Tora! Tora!* and seen at US air shows continue to be the only flying representations of the type.

ABOVE LEFT: **A Nakajima B5N1 'Kate' taking off from the Japanese aircraft carrier** *Akagi*. **Note the size of the torpedo.** ABOVE: **A B5N2 pictured over Hickam Field during the Pearl Harbor attack. The caption for this photograph when it was released in Japan read, "Pearl Harbor in flame and smoke, gasping helplessly under the severe pounding of our Sea Eagles."**

ABOVE: **As well as Pearl Harbor, the B5N was also the type that destroyed the USS** *Hornet*, *Lexington* **and** *Yorktown*. BELOW LEFT: **Although the type was withdrawn from front-line service due to increased vulnerability to Allied fighters, their contribution to Japan's war effort was immense.**

Nakajima B5N2

First flight: January 1937 (prototype)
Power: One Nakajima 1,000hp NK1B Sakae 11 engine
Armament: One flexible 7.7mm machine-gun in rear cockpit and up to 800kg/1,764lb of bombs or a torpedo
Size: Wingspan – 15.52m/50ft 11in
Length – 10.3m/33ft 9.5in
Height – 3.7m/12ft 1in
Wing area – 37.7m²/406sq ft
Weights: Empty – 2,279kg/5,024lb
Maximum take-off – 4,100kg/9,039lb
Performance: Maximum speed – 378kph/235mph
Ceiling – 8,260m/27,100ft
Range – 1,990km/1,237 miles
Climb – 3,000m/9,840ft in 7 minutes, 40 seconds

Nakajima B6N Tenzan

The Nakajima B6N Tenzan (heavenly mountain) was the Imperial Japanese Navy's standard torpedo-bomber for the final years of World War II. Codenamed 'Jill' by the Allies, the aircraft was a development of Nakajima's B5N and replaced it in service. Although the B6N was an effective torpedo-bomber, by the time it got into service the Allied air superiority in the Pacific severely limited its usefulness.

The shortcomings of the B5N were never rectified, but the Japanese Navy had high hopes for a replacement aircraft. Its 1939 specification called to for an aircraft that could carry the same weapon load as the B5N but at greater speed and over a greater range while not being any bigger than the earlier aircraft. The restriction was due to the size of carrier deck lifts. This led the designers to a novel way of creating a rudder of increased area by taking more of the fin and sloping the rudder's front edge forwards, top first.

The aircraft had no internal weapons bay and the torpedo was carried distinctively offset to the right, while the large oil cooler was offset to the left. The type's development was

ABOVE: **The B6N was evidently developed from Nakajima's earlier B5N but brought significant performance improvements for the Japanese Navy. The B6N2 version pictured was powered by the Kasei engine.**

protracted and not easy – there were stability and engine problems (vibration and overheating among others) during the early 1941 testing. This led to a two-year delay in entry to front-line service.

Tenzans went into service for the first time in late 1943, off Bougainville in the Solomon Islands. The B6N1's combat debut in the Battle of the Philippine Sea was a disaster as the US Navy's air superiority meant that the American fighters were able to inflict massive losses while disrupting the B6N1's attacks. The Japanese Navy immediately ordered improvements, the most significant of which was the replacement of the NK7A Mamori 11 engine with the Mitsubishi MK4T Kasei 25, resulting in the improved B6N2 version. The Kasei was slightly less powerful but led to a more streamlined aircraft.

LEFT: **Nakajima's B6N could fly faster and farther than the earlier B5N from which it was developed. Note the unusual and innovative fin shape that gave more control surface area without increasing the height of the fin. Such solutions were – and still are – essential in the creation of carrier-borne aircraft.**

This heavy aircraft could only operate from the largest Japanese carriers, most of which had been destroyed or put out of commission. Accordingly, most B6N2 operations took place from land bases, meaning they failed to make use of this version's improvements and lacked tactical surprise.

Although the Tenzans fought in the Battle of Okinawa, it was also here that the aircraft were used for the first time for kamikaze missions.

Towards the end of the war some were equipped with radar for night-time torpedo attacks on Allied shipping. As the Allies pressed closer to the Japanese homeland, the Japanese Navy's role shifted from attack to one of defence. Accordingly, the final version of the B6N was for land-only use and was much lighter and faster due to the lack of equipment and features previously required for carrier operations. For example, it had a strengthened undercarriage with larger tyres for rough field operations. Two of these B6N3 prototypes were completed, but Japan surrendered before this variant entered production.

A total of 1,268 B6Ns were built, the majority of them B6N2s. Today, only one survives and is preserved at the National Air and Space Museum in the United States.

TOP: **The loss of Japan's larger carriers that could carry the large B6N and the loss of experienced flight crews meant the B6N was never able to demonstrate its improved performance.** ABOVE: **The B6N can be easily identified by the way it had to carry its torpedo offset to the right due to the presence of a large oil radiator protruding under the aircraft belly.**

BELOW: **The wartime caption for this photograph taken on December 4, 1943, reads, "A Japanese Nakajima B6N 'Tenzan' torpedo-bomber explodes in the air after a direct hit by a 5in shell from USS *Yorktown* (CV-10) as it attempted an unsuccessful attack on the carrier off Kwajalein."**

Nakajima B6N2 Tenzan

First flight: 1941
Power: One Mitsubishi 1,850hp Kasei-25 14-cylinder two-row radial engine
Armament: One 7.7mm machine-gun, manually aimed, in rear cockpit, one 7.7mm machine-gun, manually aimed by middle crew member, in rear ventral position plus one torpedo or 800kg/1,746lb of bombs carried under fuselage
Size: Wingspan – 14.89m/48ft 10.5in
Length – 10.87m/35ft 8in
Height – 3.8m/12ft 5.5in
Wing area – 37.2m2/400sq ft
Weights: Empty – 3,010kg/6,636lb
Maximum take-off – 5,650kg/12,456lb
Performance: Maximum speed – 481kph/299mph
Ceiling – 9,040m/29,660ft
Range – 3,045km/1,892 miles
Climb – 5,000m/16,400ft in 10 minutes, 24 seconds

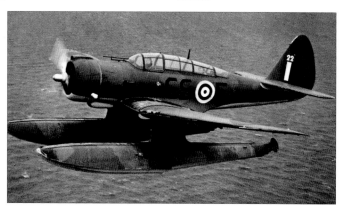

LEFT: **Another very distinctive and easy to identify aircraft, the N-3PB was the first aircraft produced by the newly formed Northrop.** ABOVE: **The two large floats gave the aircraft great stability on the water and would be fitted with beaching gear to be manoeuvred on land.** BELOW: **The N-3PB's achievements were way out of proportion to the tiny numbers of the type that were produced and saw service with Norwegian crews serving in the RAF.**

Northrop N-3PB

The Northrop N-3PB was a single-engine low-wing twin-float aircraft with a crew of three. The only customer for this rare aircraft was the Royal Norwegian Navy Air Service (RNNAS) who needed a patrol bomber to protect its waters.

Norway ordered 24 aircraft on March 12, 1940, but before the aircraft could be delivered, Norway was invaded by Germany. As a result, all of the aircraft were delivered to the exiled RNNAS which operated as No.330 (Norwegian) Squadron of RAF Coastal Command based in Reykjavik, Iceland. On May 19, 1941, 18 aircraft arrived in Iceland. Twelve N-3PBs were assembled immediately and divided among the squadron's three flights, based at Reykjavik, Akureiry in northern Iceland and Budareiry in eastern Iceland. Following the loss of ten of the aircraft (due to extreme weather), the remaining aircraft were gradually put into operation. The first operational sortie by an N-3PB was flown from Reykjavik on June 23, 1941.

The squadron moved to Scotland in August 1943 to re-equip with Sunderlands but in their time on Iceland the N-3PBs flew 1,041 operational sorties including 379 convoy-escort missions and 246 anti-U-boat missions. The squadron spotted fifteen U-boats,

attacked nine and damaged seven. N-3PBs were also credited with damage to eight enemy aircraft. These are remarkable results given the very low numbers of aircraft involved and the sheer size of their patrol areas.

On April 21, 1943, an N-3PB, call sign 'U', took off from Budareiry heading for Reykjavik. En route the crew encountered heavy snow showers and were forced to land on a glacier river. The aircraft was wrecked and sank but the crew survived. Thirty-six years later the aircraft was located, removed and restored over a period of a year by Northrop in California. This sole survivor is now preserved and displayed at a museum in Gardermoen, Norway.

Northrop N-3PB

First flight: November 1, 1940
Power: One Wright 1,100hp GR-1820-G205A Cyclone air-cooled radial engine
Armament: Four fixed forward-firing 0.5in machine-guns in wings, one 0.3in machine-gun in dorsal and ventral positions and up to 907kg/2,000lb of bombs
Size: Wingspan – 14.91m/48ft 11in
Length – 10.97m/36ft
Height – 3.66m/12ft
Wing area – 34.93m²/376sq ft
Weights: Empty – 2,808kg/6,190lb
Maximum take-off – 4,808kg/10,600lb
Performance: Maximum speed – 414kph/257mph
Ceiling – 7,392m/28,400ft
Range – 1,609km/1,000 miles
Climb – 4,572m/15,000ft in 14 minutes, 24 seconds

Parnall Peto

In 1926, Parnall were approached to produce an unusual aircraft for an even more unusual role. The specification called for a small two-seat floatplane with folding wings that could be carried in a 2.44m/8ft-wide watertight hangar on the deck of the Royal Navy submarine M.2. The project was conceived by submarine commander Sir Max Horton who believed that the future of sea power lay with submarines and aircraft and not ships.

The Peto was made of mixed wood, fabric, aluminium and steel, and had unequal span. One prototype was powered by a 135hp Bristol Lucifer engine while the second had an Armstrong Siddeley 135hp Mongoose. Six production aircraft are believed to have been ordered.

Once the submarine had surfaced, the aircraft was launched by a compressed air catapult along a short length of track. The aircraft was then supposed to scout for enemy ships, note their position, then land back near the submarine. A crane would lift the aircraft back on to its launch rails, then a winch would haul the aircraft backwards, the wings would be folded manually and the aircraft would return to its hangar with two sets of watertight doors closing behind it. The

submarine would then head to the enemy ships and launch an attack. Speed of aircraft deployment was clearly important and the crew were eager to break their 12-minute record.

On January 26, 1932, M.2 was lost with all hands. Divers found the sub on

the seabed with both hangar doors and the hatch connecting the hangar to the sub open. It is believed that the crew, eager to improve on the time taken to launch the aircraft, opened the pressure-hull hatch to the hangar as well as the watertight hangar door while the boat was still partly submerged. The water rushed in and the sub sank quickly. The experiment was never repeated by the Royal Navy and the Peto remains the first and only conventional aircraft to be launched from a British submersible aircraft carrier.

Parnall Peto

First flight: June 4, 1925
Power: One Armstrong Siddeley 135hp Mongoose IIIC 5-cylinder air-cooled radial engine
Armament: None
Size: Wingspan – 8.66m/28ft 5in
    Length – 6.86m/22ft 6in
    Height – 2.71m/8ft 11in
    Wing area – 16.17m²/174sq ft
Weights: Empty – 590kg/1,300lb
    Maximum take-off – 885kg/1,950lb
Performance: Maximum speed – 181kph/113mph
    Ceiling – 3,447m/11,300ft
    Endurance – 2 hours
    Climb – 183m/600ft per minute

Saro London

Thirty-one examples of Saro's London biplane flying boat were built for Royal Air Force Coastal Command who operated the type in the front line from 1936 until 1941. The London, with its crew of five, is another fine example of an outmoded aircraft that had to remain in service for much longer than planned as there were simply no more capable, modern aircraft available at the time.

The first flight of the London took place in 1934, the aircraft having been designed to meet a specification calling for a 'general-purpose open-sea patrol flying boat'. The London was in fact derived from Saro's earlier and larger Severn flying boat. The first ten aircraft built were Mk Is with Bristol Pegasus III engines and can be identified by the

powerplants' polygonal cowlings and two-bladed propellers. The definitive Mk II had Pegasus X engines with circular cowlings and four-bladed propellers – construction of this version continued until May 1938 with surviving Mk Is being upgraded to the II standard.

Having first entered service with No.201 Squadron in April 1936, Londons were chosen to represent the RAF on the 150th anniversary of the founding of the State of New South Wales in 1937. Five Londons equipped with auxiliary fuel tanks flew from Britain to Australia demonstrating the type's long-range capabilities over a round trip that covered 48,280km/30,000 miles.

The London was still in service at the start of World War II with Nos.201, 202

ABOVE: **The Saro London served with three RAF Coastal Command squadrons during the early part of World War II.** BELOW: **K3560 was the London prototype built to Air Ministry specification R.24/31 and was later converted to London II standard.**

and 240 Squadrons, carrying out anti-submarine duties and convoy patrols. The type was one of very few front-line biplanes still in the British inventory. It was the aircraft based at Gibraltar that served until April 1941 when they were finally replaced in service by the Consolidated Catalina.

Saro London Mk II

First flight: 1934 (prototype)
Power: Two Bristol 1,055hp Pegasus X radial piston engines
Armament: Three 0.303in machine-guns in bow and midships plus up to 907kg/2,000lb of bombs or depth charges
Size: Wingspan – 24.38m/80ft
Length – 17.31m/56ft 10in
Height – 5.72m/18ft 9in
Wing area – 132.38m²/1,425sq ft
Weights: Empty – 5,035kg/11,100lb
Maximum take-off – 8,346kg/18,400lb
Performance: Maximum speed – 249kph/155mph
Service ceiling – 6,065m/19,900ft
Range – 2,800km/1,740 miles
Climb – 360m/1,180ft per minute

LEFT: **Looking like a flying wing on a pair of pontoons, the S.55 was revolutionary in terms of flying boat configuration.** ABOVE: **The 24 S.55s prepare to take off for the Balbo-led transatlantic flight – a remarkable feat of airmanship even by today's standards.**

Savoia-Marchetti S.55

Savoia-Marchetti's S.55 must surely be the most distinctive flying boat in aviation history. The S.55 was proposed to meet an Italian military requirement for a large long-range multi-engine torpedo/bomber flying boat that could carry a substantial bomb load. It first flew in 1924 and encapsulated its designers' daring, ingenuity and advanced understanding of aero- and hydrodynamics. It was a monoplane with twin catamaran-type hulls and two fins and three rudders connected to the rest of the aircraft by two of the stripped-down booms. The two pilots sat side by side in open cockpits located in the leading edge of the centre of the wing. Twin tandem engines, one tractor, one pusher, were mounted on struts over the wing and canted sharply at an upward

angle. It must be borne in mind that this aircraft appeared only seven years after the end of World War I in an era dominated by biplanes.

Engine power was gradually increased from the 300hp of the prototype's engines to the 880hp of later versions' engines. However, the Italian Navy were initially unimpressed by the prototype's poor performance and were suspicious of the aircraft's unusual configuration. The manufacturers persevered and developed a civil version, the S.55C which could accommodate five passengers in each of the two hulls. This rekindled the military's interest and the first military orders followed.

The S.55 earned worldwide fame through spectacular long-distance flights. Lt Col the Marchese de Pinedo

flew an S.55 named *Santa Maria* from Sardinia to Buenos Aires and then through South America and the USA and back to Italy, covering a distance of nearly 48,280km/30,000 miles. The S.55 will perhaps be best remembered, however, for the remarkable mass formation flights led by the senior Italian Air Force officer Italo Balbo who led fleets of S.55s across the Atlantic. In 1933 he led 24 aircraft all the way to the US and Chicago's Century of Progress International Exposition, flying all the way in a tight 'v' formation.

The type went on to equip numerous Italian long-range maritime reconnaissance/bomber units and some of the machines were still in reserve when World War II broke out. Total production of civil and military versions exceeded 200.

LEFT: **One of the Balbo-flight aircraft being prepared for the transatlantic flight. Note the angle of the engine 'pod'. The flight made the S.55 world famous. Only one example of an S.55 survives, currently under restoration in Sao Paolo, Brazil.**

Savoia-Marchetti S.55X

First flight: August 1924 (prototype)
Power: Two 880hp Isotta-Fraschini Asso 750 Vee piston engines
Armament: Four 7.7mm machine-guns plus one torpedo or up to 2,000kg/4,409lb of bombs
Size: Wingspan – 24m/78ft 9in
  Length – 16.75m/54ft 11.5in
  Height – 5m/16ft 4.75in
  Wing area – 93m^2/1,001sq ft
Weights: Empty – 5,750kg/12,677lb
  Maximum take-off – 8,260kg/18,210lb
Performance: Maximum speed – 279kph/173mph
  Ceiling – 5,000m/16,405ft
  Range – 3,500km/2,175 miles

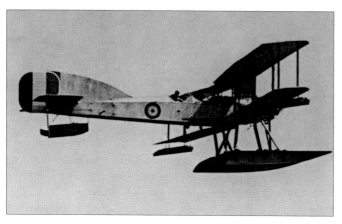

Short Type 184

The Short Type 184 was designed by Horace Short to meet an urgent requirement from the British Admiralty for a torpedo-carrying seaplane. The first example flew at Rochester in early 1915 powered by a 225hp Sunbeam Maori engine. By the end of an impressive production run of 936, involving Short Brothers and nine other aircraft manufacturers, the '184' had established itself as the company's most successful inter-war type.

On August 12, 1915, a Short 184 operating from the seaplane carrier HMS *Ben-My-Chree* in the Aegean became the first aircraft in the world to attack an enemy ship with an air-launched torpedo. Piloted by Flight Commander Charles H.K. Edmonds, the aircraft dropped a 367kg/810lb torpedo against a 5,000-ton Turkish supply ship which

subsequently sank, although a British submarine commander also claimed the victory. On August 17, however, Edmonds torpedoed a Turkish steamer a few miles north of the Dardanelles and on this occasion there was no dispute as to how the vessel had been destroyed.

Another Short 184 from Edmond's flight on the same mission had to put down on the sea due to engine problems. The pilot, Flight Lieutenant G.B. Dacre, spotted an enemy tug nearby and nursed the aircraft engine to give enough power for him to taxi nearer to the tug. Dacre then dropped his torpedo into the sea from zero feet – it ran true and sank the enemy ship.

These early torpedo successes were, however, not typical and the type came to be used more for bombing and reconnaissance. The aircraft went on to

ABOVE LEFT: **The Type 184 is assured of its place in the history books thanks to the August 1915 torpedo attacks by Flight Commander Edmonds.**
ABOVE: **The bravery of the pioneering naval aviators is well illustrated in this study. Note the open cockpit and the exposed construction of the aircraft.**

serve in most theatres during World War I. Wheels could be added to the floats to allow take-off from the decks of carrier aircraft. When the RAF was formed in April 1918 from the RFC and the RNAS, the RAF took over most of the RNAS 184s and the type continued to protect Britain's coastline and its interests overseas into 1920.

A landplane version of the Short 184 was sold to the Royal Flying Corps as the Short Bomber. A forward fuselage section of a Short 184 is preserved by the Fleet Air Arm Museum in the UK.

Short Type 184

First flight: Spring 1915
Power: One Sunbeam 260hp Maori Vee engine
Armament: One 0.303in machine-gun in rear cockpit plus one 356mm/14in torpedo or up to 236kg/520lb of bombs
Size: Wingspan – 19.36m/63ft 6.25in
  Length – 12.38m/40ft 8in
  Height – 4.11m/13ft
  Wing area – 63.92m²/688sq ft
Weights: Empty – 1,680kg/3,703lb
  Maximum take-off – 2,433kg/5,363lb
Performance: Maximum speed – 142kph/88mph
  Ceiling – 2,745m/9,000ft
  Endurance – 2 hours, 45 minutes
  Climb – 610m/2,000ft in 8 minutes, 35 seconds

ABOVE: **HMS *Engadine* was a World War I Royal Navy seaplane tender. Built as a Folkestone-Boulogne ferry, *Engadine* was taken over by the Navy in 1914, and cranes and a hangar were added for operating four Short 184 seaplanes.**

Short Singapore III

The Short Singapore was the last of a number of biplane flying boats built by the company and the last use of the name that was first applied to the record-breaking Singapore I of 1926. The Singapore III became a vital element of the Royal Air Force's flying boat force in Britain and overseas in the years leading up to World War II.

The four-engined Short S.12 Singapore II of 1930 was a triple-finned development of the Singapore I but its powerplants were arranged in twin tandem configuration. The four engines were arranged in tandem pairs with two pushing and two pulling. Although this version did not enter production, the Air Ministry was interested enough to order four development flying boats based on the Singapore II. These aircraft, trialled at the Marine Aircraft Experimental Establishment, became the pre-production Singapore Mk IIIs.

The production aircraft that followed were built to Air Ministry specification R.14/34 and the first production example, K3592, first flew on June 15, 1934. Production continued until mid-1937 by which time 37 aircraft had been produced for the Royal Air Force.

The Singapore III, with a crew of six, had all-metal hulls, fabric-covered metal flying surfaces and was powered by four 675hp Rolls-Royce Kestrel IX engines

mounted between the wings. If required, an auxiliary long-range fuel tank could be carried externally on the dorsal hull.

The first RAF unit to operate the type was No.210 Squadron at Pembroke Dock while the first overseas deployment came in April 1935 with No.205 Squadron in Singapore.

By the time this large biplane entered RAF service it was effectively obsolete but it did significantly increase the RAF's flying boat fleet during the mid-1930s arms race. Despite the age of its basic design, 19 Singapore IIIs were still in RAF service when World War II broke out, based in the UK, Aden and Singapore. It was at the latter location that, appropriately, the Singapore III soldiered on until being withdrawn in October 1941. Four of these aircraft were passed to No.5 Squadron of the Royal New Zealand Air Force for use in Fiji and saw action during which a Japanese submarine was destroyed. The Singapores were finally replaced by Consolidated Catalinas.

TOP: **The Singapore III was arrived at through a series of configuration experiments and trials. This aircraft is a Singapore II with a single fin pictured in 1930.** ABOVE LEFT: **This view of two Singapore IIIs show the distinctive triple fin arrangement and the scale of the type. Note the very streamlined engine 'pod' arrangement.** ABOVE: **This enhanced publicity shot from the early 1930s shows a Singapore being put through its paces at low level.**

Short Singapore III

First flight: June 15, 1934 (production Singapore III)
Power: Four Rolls-Royce 730hp Kestrel X radial engines
Armament: Three 0.303in machine-guns in bow, dorsal and tail positions plus up to 907kg/2,000lb of bombs
Size: Wingspan – 27.4m/90ft
    Length – 19.5m/64ft 2in
    Height – 7.01m/23ft 7in
    Wing area – 170.5m²/1,834sq ft
Weights: Empty – 8,360kg/18,420lb
    Maximum take-off – 14,300kg/31,500lb
Performance: Maximum speed – 233kph/145mph
    Ceiling – 4,570m/15,000ft
    Range – 1,609km/1,000 miles
    Climb – 213m/700ft per minute

Short Sunderland

The Sunderland is one of only a handful of military aircraft that were developed from an existing civil type. Based upon Shorts' C-Class 'Empire' flying boats operated by Imperial Airways in the 1930s, the Short Sunderland became one of the Royal Air Force's longest-serving operational aircraft over the next two decades. Its service during World War II and, specifically, the Sunderland's decisive role in the defeat of German U-boats in the Battle of the Atlantic, marks it as one of aviation history's finest ever flying boats. Although the first flight of the prototype Sunderland took place in October 1937, the Air Ministry were already familiar with the aircraft's successful civilian counterpart and had placed an order in March the preceding year.

During June 1938 No.230 Squadron, based in Singapore, received the first service delivery of production Sunderland Mk Is. When the Sunderland joined the RAF inventory and replaced the RAF's mixed fleet of biplane flying boats, it represented a huge leap in capability.

ABOVE: **The Sunderland cockpit area was roomy and offered the aircraft's crew excellent visibility. In hot climates the crew had to be careful to avoid sunstroke due to the cockpit's extensive glazing.**

TOP: **The very capable Sunderland enabled the wartime Royal Air Force to project its reach over vast expanses of ocean.** ABOVE: **This excellent side view of a 'beached' Sunderland III shows the version's new planing bottom in which the forward step was made shallower. This aircraft, W3999, was the first production example of the Mk III.**

By the outbreak of World War II in September 1939 three RAF Coastal Command squadrons had become operational and were ready to seek out and destroy German submarines. The Sunderland also became a very welcome sight to the many seamen from sunken vessels and the airmen who had ditched out over the ocean. This is best illustrated by the tale of the British merchant ship *Kensington Court*. It had been torpedoed 112km/70 miles off the Isles of Scilly on September 18, 1939, but two patrolling Sunderlands had the entire crew of 34 back on dry land just an hour after the ship sank.

The Sunderland, with its crew of ten, heavily armed and bristling with machine-guns, became known to the Luftwaffe as the 'Flying Porcupine'. Many times during the war a lone Sunderland fought off or defeated a number of attacking aircraft.

Although Sunderlands did engage in many a 'shoot-out' with German vessels, sometimes the sight of the large and well-armed aircraft was enough to have an enemy crew scuttle their boat – such was the case on January 31, 1940, when the arrival

of a Sunderland from No.228 Squadron prompted the crew of U-Boat *U-55* to do just that.

The Sunderland Mk II was introduced at the end of 1940, powered by four Pegasus XVIII engines with two-stage superchargers, a twin-gun dorsal turret, an improved rear turret and Air-to-Surface-Vessel (ASV) Mk II radar. The most numerous version was the Mk III that first flew in December 1941. This variant had a modified hull for improved planing when taking off. This was followed by a larger and heavier version designated the Mk IV/Seaford. However, after evaluation by the RAF the project was abandoned.

The Mk V was the ultimate version of the Sunderland and made its appearance at the end of 1943. It was powered by four 1,200hp Pratt & Whitney R-1830-90 Twin Wasp engines and carried ASV Mk VI radar. By the end of the final production run in 1945, a total of 739 Sunderlands had been built and after World War II, many continued to serve with the British, French, Australian, South African and New Zealand air forces.

ABOVE: **The Royal New Zealand Air Force were just one of the Sunderland's post-war operators. The RNZAF aircraft were not retired until 1967, three decades after the prototype first flew.**

Post-war, RAF Sunderlands delivered nearly 5,000 tons of supplies during the Berlin Airlift, and during the Korean War Sunderlands were the only British aircraft to operate throughout the war. During the Malayan Emergency RAF Sunderlands carried out bombing raids against terrorist camps.

The Sunderland finally retired from the Royal Air Force on May 15, 1959, when No.205 Squadron flew the last sortie for the type from RAF Changi, Singapore, where the illustrious operational career of the Sunderland flying boat had begun over two decades earlier. It was, however, the Royal New Zealand Air Force who in March 1967 became the last air arm to retire the type from military service.

Between 1937 and 1946 a total of 749 Sunderlands were built – this included 240 built at Blackburn's Dumbarton plant.

ABOVE: **The Short Sunderland offered Allied convoys excellent protection within its range, and was a major weapon against the 'U-boat menace' in the war for the Atlantic.**

Short Sunderland Mk V

First flight: October 16, 1937 (prototype)
Power: Four Pratt & Whitney 1,200hp R-1830 Twin Wasp 14-cylinder air-cooled radials
Armament: Eight 0.303in Browning machine-guns in turrets, four fixed 0.303in Browning machine-guns in nose, two manually operated 0.5in machine-guns in beam positions and 2,250kg/4,960lb of depth charges or bombs
Size: Wingspan – 34.36m/112ft 9in
Length – 26m/85ft 3in
Height – 10.01m/32ft 11in
Wing area – 138.14m²/1,487sq ft
Weights: Empty – 16,783kg/37,000lb
Maximum take-off – 27,216kg/60,000lb
Performance: Maximum speed – 343kph/213mph
Ceiling – 5,456m/17,900ft
Range – 4,785km/2,980 miles
Climb – 256m/840ft per minute

Sopwith Camel

The Sopwith Camel, which evolved from the Sopwith Pup and Sopwith Triplane, is the best-known British aircraft of World War I. Credited with the destruction of around 3,000 enemy aircraft, it was by far the most effective fighter of World War I. The aircraft was very easy to turn due to its forward-placed centre of gravity, a result of the concentration of the engine, armament, pilot and fuel in the front 2.17m/7ft of the fuselage. This, coupled with its very sensitive controls, made the aircraft something of a handful for inexperienced pilots but in skilled hands the Camel was an excellent fighter and virtually unbeatable. Like the Pup, the Sopwith Biplane F.1 became better known by its nickname, in this case the 'Camel', and the aircraft's official designation is largely forgotten.

The prototype, powered by a 110hp Clerget 9Z, first flew at Brooklands in February 1917 and was followed by the F.1/3 pre-production model. First deliveries went to Royal Naval Air Service No.4 (Naval) Squadron at Dunkirk who received their new fighter in June 1917. The first Camel air victory occurred

TOP: **The Camel is among the most famous fighter aircraft ever built and its capabilities inevitably led to naval aviation applications.** ABOVE: **HMAS Sydney was attacked by a Zeppelin during May 1917 which escaped unscathed. The Captain was keen to not let an enemy escape again, so a flying platform for launching aircraft was built on the ship. Here a Camel is seen being launched from a gun platform.**

ABOVE: **A Camel being launched from HMS Tiger, which was one of a number of Royal Navy ships modified to launch aircraft. Note the tail's high attitude to ease a swift take-off.**

within days when, on June 4, Flight Commander A.M. Shook sent a German aircraft down into the sea – on the next day Shook attacked 15 enemy aircraft and is believed to have destroyed 2 of them. The Royal Flying Corps' first Camel victory was achieved by Captain C. Collett on June 27.

One manoeuvre, unique to the Camel, was an incredibly quick starboard turn assisted by the torque of its big rotary engine. So fast was the right turn that pilots were able to use it to great advantage in combat, sometimes choosing to make three-quarter right turns in place of the slower quarter turn to the left. It was risky though as during the sharp right turns, the nose tried to go violently downwards due to the torque of the engine. Camels were built with a variety of engines including the Clerget 9B, Bentley BR1, Gnome Monosoupape and Le Rhône 9J.

In the Battle of Cambrai in March 1918, Captain J.L. Trollope of No.43 Squadron used his Camel to shoot down six enemy aircraft in one day – March 24. Later that year, Camels were in the thick of what many historians believe to be the greatest dogfight of World War I. On the morning of November 4, 1918,

Camels of Nos.65 and 204 Squadrons attacked 40 Fokker DVIIs. The pilots of No.56 claimed eight destroyed, six out of control and one driven down, while the pilots of 204 claimed two destroyed and five out of control. Perhaps the most famous single Camel victory is, however, that of Canadian Camel pilot Roy Brown who was credited with the death of Manfred von Richthofen, the Red Baron, on April 21, 1918.

By the end of 1917, over 1,000 Camels were delivered and work began on subvariants including naval versions. Those specially designed for shipboard use were designated the 2F.1 Camel and were the last type of Camel built. The majority were powered by BR.1 rotary engines and most were armed with one Lewis and one Vickers machine-gun – some carried two 22.7kg/50lb bombs on underwing bomb racks. Sea-going Camels had a slightly reduced wingspan and a completely removable tail for easy stowage. They also differed from land-based Camels by having jettisonable tubular-steel landing gear. These versions were flown from Royal Navy aircraft carriers HMS *Furious* and *Pegasus* but were also launched, or more accurately, catapulted, from platforms built on the gun turrets or forecastles of other British fighting ships of the time. In July 1918, 2F.1 Camels took off from HMS *Furious* in the North Sea and flew into the mouth of the River Elbe where they attacked and bombed enemy airship sheds at Tondern. Despite being

fighters, these nimble aircraft became bombers credited with the destruction of Zeppelins *L54* and *L60*. By the Armistice in November 1918, Britain's Grand Fleet had 112 2F.1s in its inventory. Post-war, six Camels that had served with US Navy squadrons in France during hostilities were shipped to the US for platform-launching trials aboard USS *Texas* and *Arkansas*.

In addition to the RFC, RNAS and RAF, Camels were also operated by Belgium, Canada, Greece and the air force of the American Expeditionary Force. Total Camel production was around 5,500.

ABOVE: Camels operating from ships would sometimes have to put down in the water. This was a hazardous operation for the pilot.

Sopwith F1. Camel

First flight: February 26, 1917
Power: Clerget 130hp 9-cylinder air-cooled rotary piston engine
Armament: Two 0.303in synchronized Vickers machine-guns on nose, plus four 11.35kg/25lb bombs carried below fuselage
Size: Wingspan – 8.53m/28ft
Length – 5.72m/18ft 9in
Height – 2.6m/8ft 6in
Wing area – 21.46m²/231sq ft
Weights: Empty – 421kg/929lb
Maximum take-off – 659kg/1,453lb
Performance: Maximum speed – 188kph/117mph
Ceiling – 5,790m/19,000ft
Endurance – 2 hours, 30 minutes
Climb – 3,050m/10,000ft in 10 minutes, 35 seconds

ABOVE: Shipborne Royal Navy Camels carried out audacious and hard-hitting raids that showed, even at this early stage, just how useful and effective shipborne air power could be.

Supermarine Scapa and Stranraer

Supermarine developed the Supermarine Southampton Mk IV – an upgraded, modernized and re-engined version – from the trusty Southampton design in response to Air Ministry specification R.20/31. It first flew on July 8, 1934, with 'Mutt' Summers at the controls and by October the following year it had been renamed the Scapa. While the Scapa was the same size as the aircraft from which it was developed, it contained many changes and modifications. Although the fuselage retained the same broad profile, the Scapa introduced twin fins and rudders in place of the three used on the Southampton. Much to the pilots' delight, the Scapa introduced a side-by-side enclosed cockpit. The all-metal Scapa featured aerodynamically neat, cowled Rolls-Royce Kestrels. Fourteen production aircraft were built for the RAF, the last of which were delivered by July 1936. Nos.202 and 204 Squadrons, operating from Malta and Aboukir/

Alexandria respectively, operated the type on anti-submarine patrols protecting neutral shipping during the Spanish Civil War. The Scapa was able to demonstrate its long-range capabilities on some high-profile publicity flights including a 14,480km/9000-mile return cruise to Africa. The type was gradually replaced in service, the last being retired by the close of 1938.

A related development was the Supermarine Stranraer, originally known as the Southampton V. This was the last biplane flying boat created by R.J. Mitchell and was a larger derivative with a wingspan almost 3m/10ft greater than the Scapa as well as a longer fuselage. It acquired the name Stranraer in August 1935, having first flown in July 1934. This aircraft also differed from the Scapa by having a gun position in the tail for self-defence.

Seventeen Stranraers were ordered by the Air Ministry in August 1935 and the type first entered RAF service with

ABOVE: **The Supermarine Stranraer remained in Royal Air Force service when World War II began.**
BELOW LEFT: **The record-breaking Scapa was aerodynamically refined for its day with its engines in neat 'pods'.**

No.228 Squadron in April 1937. The type was used exclusively around the coast of the UK by RAF Coastal Command. When World War II broke out in September 1939, 15 Stranraers were still in service and continued to serve well into 1941 until being replaced by Consolidated Catalinas.

The Royal Canadian Air Force also operated Stranraers throughout World War II – these 40 machines were licence-built by Canadian Vickers in Montreal, and a number entered civil use after the war's end.

Supermarine Stranraer

First flight: July 27, 1934 (prototype Southampton V)
Power: Two Bristol 875hp Pegasus X radial piston engine
Armament: Three 0.303in machine-guns in nose, dorsal and tail positions
Size: Wingspan – 25.91m/85ft
    Length – 16.71m/54ft 10in
    Height – 6.63m/21ft 9in
    Wing area – 135.36m²/1,457sq ft
Weights: Empty – 5,103kg/11,250lb
    Maximum take-off – 8,618kg/19,000lb
Performance: Maximum speed – 268kph/165mph
    Ceiling – 5,639m/18,500ft
    Range – 1,609km/1,000 miles
    Climb – 411m/1,350ft per minute

LEFT: **Derived from a civil aircraft, the Southampton became an important means of demonstrating long-range British military reach around its Empire.**
BELOW LEFT: **When the Southampton's old wooden hull was replaced with a lightweight metal one, the change significantly altered the aircraft's performance for the better.**

Supermarine Southampton

Felixstowe flying boats had been in RAF service since World War I and were rather long in the tooth by the mid-1920s. Their replacement, the Supermarine Southampton, was one of the RAF's most successful ever flying boats. The type was the first flying boat designed after World War I to enter RAF service but was in fact derived from a civilian flying boat, the Supermarine Swan. The success of the Swan gave the Air Ministry the confidence to order six of the military version straight from the drawing board.

It was also the first successful design led by R.J. Mitchell who went on to design the legendary Spitfire which was itself derived from a high-speed floatplane. It was the Southampton biplane that brought to prominence the name of the designer and the company that employed him.

The first production version was the Southampton Mk I, of which 24 were built with wooden hulls and wings. This was followed into service by 41 examples of the Mk II with lightweight metal hulls and the more powerful Lion VA engines. Later Mk IIs had slightly swept-back outer wing sections but all had underwing stabilizing floats and a distinctive tail with three fins and rudders. Its engines were mounted between the wings.

By 1933 the earlier wooden-hulled machines were eventually all reassembled with metal hulls. The duralumin hull was not only structurally lighter than wood but the wooden hull also carried an additional 181kg/400lb in the weight of the water that the wood absorbed. The weight-saving of the metal hull appreciably improved performance, which equated to an additional 325km/200-mile range.

The type first entered RAF service in August 1925 with No.480 Coastal Reconnaissance Flight. The Southampton was soon known as a record-breaker after carrying out a 16,000km/10,000-mile cruise around the British Isles, demonstrating the type's reliability and endurance. In 1926,

two aircraft flew from the UK's south coast to Egypt on an 11,270km/7,000-mile round trip.

The Southamptons became synonymous with 'flying the flag' and went on to carry out a four-ship cruise from Felixstowe to Singapore via the Mediterranean and India in 1927 and 1928. This cruise covered no less than 43,500km/27,000 miles.

The popular and reliable Southampton served the RAF for over a decade, retiring in December 1936 – the type was also exported to Argentina, Australia (RAAF), Japan and Turkey.

One Southampton survives, a Mk I, registration N9899, preserved at the Royal Air Force Museum, Hendon.

Supermarine Southampton II

First flight: March 10, 1925 (Mk I)
Power: Two Napier 660hp Lion VA W-12 piston engines
Armament: Three 0.303in machine-guns in bow and mid positions plus up to 499kg/1,100lb of bombs
Size: Wingspan – 22.86m/75ft
    Length – 15.58m/51ft 1.5in
    Height – 6.82m/22ft 4.5in
    Wing area – 134.61m²/1,449sq ft
Weights: Empty – 4,082kg/9,000lb
    Maximum take-off – 6,895kg/15,200lb
Performance: Maximum speed – 174kph/108mph
    Ceiling – 4,265m/14,000ft
    Range – 1,497km/930 miles
    Climb – 186m/610ft per minute

LEFT: **When the Sea Otter was retired from military use, a number passed into civil use around the world – two were operated by the airline Quantas.**
ABOVE: **Royal Navy Sea Otters served until 1952, some years after RAF retirement.**

Supermarine Sea Otter

The Supermarine Sea Otter was a biplane amphibian designed to replace the Supermarine Walrus in reconnaissance and search-and-rescue duties – it became the last front-line biplane in Royal Air Force service. It was also the last biplane to enter RAF service in any capacity. The aircraft was designed to Air Ministry specification S.7/38 and was to be called the Stingray.

The prototype, K8854, first flew on September 29, 1938, and was modified after some service trials. The Sea Otter had a tractor propeller arrangement compared to the pusher configuration of the earlier Walrus. The Sea Otter was faster than its predecessor, could fly farther, handled better on the water and had a metal hull.

Production was carried out by British flying boat pioneers Saunders-Roe who acted as subcontractors to Supermarine for this project. Due to the need to build fighters and bombers first, the first production Sea Otters did not appear until January 1943, but the type did remain in production until July 1946 by which time 290 had been built.

The first Sea Otter unit was No.277 Squadron who received their aircraft later in 1943. Royal Navy Sea Otters entered service a year later and operated from land bases and carriers.

Once the Second World War was over, the Sea Otter was soon retired from RAF service although Fleet Air Arm examples remained in service until January 1952. Of 290 built, 141 served with the Royal Air Force.

Two versions were built – the amphibious Mk I that carried bombs and depth charges, and the Sea Otter ASR Mk II air-sea rescue version of which 40 were built.

The only surviving 'relic' of the type is a nose section of a Sea Otter, a piece of an ex-Royal Australian Navy machine now preserved in an Australian museum.

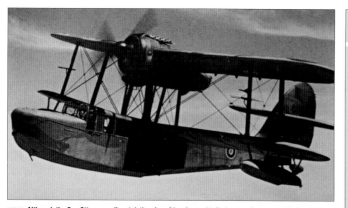

ABOVE: **Although the Sea Otter was all metal, the aircraft's wing and tail plane surfaces were fabric-covered. Note the small rudder beneath the tail, for additional control on water.**

Supermarine Sea Otter II

First flight: September 29, 1938
Power: One Bristol 855hp Mercury XXX radial piston engine
Armament: Two 0.303in machine-guns in dorsal position and one in the nose
Size: Wingspan – 14.02m/46ft
Length – 11.94m/39ft 2in
Height – 4.93m/16ft 2in
Wing area – 56.67m²/610sq ft
Weights: Empty – 3,087kg/6,805lb
Maximum take-off – 4,912kg/10,830lb
Performance: Maximum speed – 241kph/150mph
Ceiling – 4,877m/16,000ft
Range – 1,167km/725 miles
Climb – 265m/870ft per minute

LEFT: **The Walrus was a hard-working naval aircraft with a benign appearance that in fact destroyed a number of enemy craft during the war. Notice the undercarriage and the 'pusher' engine.**
BELOW: **With folding wings, the Walrus could be carried by most of the larger Royal Navy fighting ships.**

Supermarine Walrus

The amphibian Walrus was designed in 1933 by the creator of the Spitfire, R.J. Mitchell, as an improved Supermarine Seagull, incorporating a pusher instead of a tractor propeller. The prototype was designated Seagull V (though was little like the earlier Seagulls that served with the Fleet Air Arm except in name) and was built as a private venture which became the production model for the Royal Australian Air Force, the type's first customer, who took the type into service in 1935. The aircraft were to be launched from warships either by catapult or craned into the sea for take-off, then craned back on board on return from reconnaissance or air-sea rescue missions. To save space on deck, the aircraft's wings could be folded on ship reducing its storage width to just 5.5m/17ft 11in.

The Seagull was the first amphibious aircraft with a full military load to be catapult launched so it was very strong. The Walrus was popular with its crews and had a reputation for its ability to absorb battle damage. It could also be looped.

When the type entered Fleet Air Arm service in 1936, it was renamed Walrus Mk I but was better known to its crews by the nickname 'shagbat'. It was in October 1941 that the type began its RAF career as an air-sea rescue aircraft.

The Walrus served widely during World War II in the rescue and reconnaissance roles, and in East Africa as an anti-submarine bomber aircraft fitted with ASV radar. At least five enemy submarines were sunk or damaged by the seemingly harmless Walrus during World War II.

The Walrus had an unusual cockpit arrangement in that the pilot's control column was not fixed in the normal manner but could be unplugged from sockets in the floor, one in front of the pilot and co-pilot positions. Crews often

ABOVE: **The Supermarine Walrus was a very welcome sight to many hundreds of downed airmen and sailors who found themselves in distress.**

flew with just one control column then unplugged it and passed the column over while in flight. The type was retired from RAF service in April 1946.

A total of 765 Walruses including 26 Seagull Vs were built between 1936 and 1944. Only three Walruses/Seagulls still exist – one each in the UK's Fleet Air Arm Museum and RAF Museum and a further example in the RAAF Museum in Australia.

Supermarine Walrus II

First flight: June 21, 1933 (Seagull V prototype)
Power: One 775hp Bristol Pegasus VI
Armament: One 0.303in machine-gun in dorsal and nose position and up to 227kg/500lb of bombs or depth charges
Size: Wingspan – 13.97m/45ft 10in
Length – 11.45m/47ft 7in
Height – 4.65m/15ft 3in
Wing area – 56.67m²/610sq ft
Weights: Empty – 2,223kg/4,900lb
Maximum take-off – 3,266kg/7,200lb
Performance: Maximum speed – 217kph/135mph
Ceiling – 5,639m/18,500ft
Range – 965km/600 miles
Climb – 320m/1,050ft per minute

LEFT: **An experimental Spitfire Mk IX floatplane intended for Pacific service but never used.**
ABOVE: **A Mk III Seafire. The Spitfire was not a natural carrier aircraft due to poor pilot visibility and the airframe's comparative weakness.**

Supermarine Seafire

The Supermarine Seafire (initially officially known as the Sea Spitfire) was a naval version of the legendary Spitfire developed mainly for aircraft carrier operations. The sea-going Spitfire differed from its land-based cousin by features including an arrester hook in the tail, carrier catapult attachments and, in later versions, folding wings. The Seafire was not an ideal carrier fighter – it had a short range and landings were particularly challenging for pilots – but its performance, particularly its fast climb, outweighed the shortcomings.

In 1938, with war looking likely, Supermarine proposed a specifically designed naval version of the Spitfire to the Admiralty who instead decided to order the Fairey Fulmar. Three years later in September 1941, and following some disagreements about production priorities between the Admiralty and the Air Ministry, the first order for 250 examples of the most up-to-date Spitfire versions (Mks VA and B) for

the Royal Navy was placed in September 1941, and were renamed Seafire IIs.

Spitfire landing gear, designed for steady, controlled touchdowns on land, frequently collapsed as they thumped down on decks, while bouncing arrester hooks could distort the aircraft's structure. More Seafires were written off by landing incidents than by enemy action.

More ex-RAF machines were converted to improved (although chronologically confusing) Seafire Mk IB standard with naval radios and a strengthened rear fuselage with arrester hooks and slinging points. The first carrier landing of a true Seafire took place on board HMS *Illustrious* on February 10, 1942.

The Seafire F III was the next major production version and began to enter service in November 1943. This was the first Seafire version with a folding wing for easier below-deck stowage. The FIII saw most of its action in the Indian Ocean

LEFT: **Despite the aircraft's shortcomings for carrier-borne operations, the Spitfire's short-range high performance plugged a gap in the Royal Navy fighter inventory until other types were available.**

with the Far Eastern Fleet and in the Pacific with the British Pacific Fleet. It was a Seafire III that became the first aircraft of the Fleet Air Arm to fly over Japan in the summer of 1945. The Mk F IIIs were soon replaced by the low-altitude Mk LIII version powered by the Merlin 55 M engine optimized for low-level performance. Fighter reconnaissance versions also appeared armed with cameras as well as guns.

May 1945 saw the service introduction of the first Seafire version powered by the Rolls-Royce Griffon, the Seafire XV, designed from the outset with folding wings. Something of a hybrid, the XV combined the wing of the Seafire III with the fuselage of the Spitfire V and the engine, cowling and propeller of the Spitfire XII. Four Fleet Air Arm squadrons were equipped by this version at the end of World War II but it arrived too late to see action.

The first major combats involving Seafires were Operation 'Torch' in North Africa and Operation 'Husky' in Sicily. During Operation 'Torch' the first Seafire air-to-air victory was achieved by Sub Lt G.C. Baldwin. Operation 'Husky' well illustrates the fragility of the type as over 50 were lost in the first 48 hours in landing accidents.

Around D-Day the Seafire played a major gun-spotting role and subsequently supported the invasion advances. On the other side of the world, a Royal Navy Seafire claimed the last enemy aircraft to be shot down on the very day of the Japanese surrender in August 1945.

The Royal Canadian Navy bought the type as an export and French Seafires of Flotille 1F aboard the *Arromanches* saw action in the Indochina War in 1947–49. It was the ultimate version of the Seafire, the Mk 47, that saw action with the Royal Navy in Korea. The Mk 47s were able to carry three 227kg/500lb bombs or eight rockets and were 160kph/100mph faster and 2,268kg/5,000lb heavier than the first versions of the type.

The Seafire was withdrawn from front-line Fleet Air Arm service in 1951 but continued to serve with the Royal Navy Volunteer Reserve until late 1954.

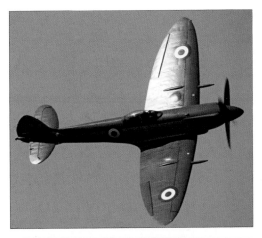

TOP: **A very rare airworthy Seafire Mk XVII, SX336, is preserved in the UK and makes frequent air show appearances. This particular aircraft first flew in 1946 and was returned to the air 60 years later.**

ABOVE: **Royal Navy Seafire FR.47s saw a lot of action in the ground-attack role in the early stages of the Korean War.**

Supermarine Seafire LF Mk III

First flight: March 5, 1936 (Spitfire prototype)
Power: One Rolls-Royce 1,583hp Merlin 55M piston engine
Armament: Two 20mm cannon, four 0.303in machine-guns and provision for up to 227kg/500lb of bombs or eight 27kg/60lb rocket projectiles
Size: Wingspan – 11.22m/36ft 10in
Length – 9.11m/29ft 11in
Height – 3.02m/9ft 11in
Wing area – 21.46m²/231sq ft
Weights: Empty – 2,472kg/5,450lb
Maximum take-off – 3,900kg/8,600lb
Performance: Maximum speed – 549kph/341mph
Service ceiling – 9,754m/32,000ft
Range – 1,239km/770 miles
Climb – 990m/3,250ft per minute

ABOVE: **A Seafire immediately following a landing accident on a Royal Navy carrier. More of the naval development of the Spitfire was lost this way than to enemy action.**

LEFT: **Pictured at a UK air show, this line-up of Corsairs show how many of the high-performance fighters are still preserved in flying condition.**
ABOVE: **A Royal Navy Corsair about to take off. The designers of the Corsair used the most powerful engine available to them at the time**
BELOW: **The 'Whistling Death' was the first Allied aircraft with the capability to halt the previously might Zero in combat.**

Vought F4U Corsair

The Corsair was not only a great naval aircraft – it was undoubtedly one of the greatest ever fighters. Designers Igor Sikorsky and Rex Beisel used the most powerful engine – a 2,000hp Pratt & Whitney R-2800 Double Wasp – and the largest propeller ever fitted to a fighter aircraft. Accordingly it was no surprise when, in 1940, the prototype Corsair exceeded 640kph/400mph, the first American combat aircraft to do so. It was equipped with a variety of armament over its long career but the Corsair was originally designed to carry two wing and two fuselage guns. Six 0.5in Browning machine-guns became standard, carried in the outer section of the wings, which folded. Cannon and rockets were later added to the weapon options.

ABOVE: **The silver XF4U-1 took to the air for the first time on May 29, 1940, at Stratford, with Vought-Sikorsky test pilot Lyman A. Bullard Jr at the controls.**

However, despite going on to be one of the fastest and most powerful fighters of World War II, the Corsair was initially rejected by the US Navy who considered it unsuitable for carrier operations. Poor cockpit visibility and a tendency to bounce on landing meant that, in February 1943 over Guadalcanal, the US Marines Corps (USMC) got the first chance to use the formidable fighter in action but as a land-based aircraft. It swiftly established itself as an excellent combat aircraft and the first Allied fighter able to take on the Japanese Zero on equal terms. The Corsair so impressed the USMC that all Marine squadrons re-equipped with the type within six months of its debut. Marine Corsair pilot Major Gregory 'Pappy' Boyington became the Corps' highest scoring pilot, ending the war with a total of 28 victories.

By the end of 1943, the mighty bent-wing fighter, operating purely from land, had accounted for over 500 Japanese aircraft. Japanese troops nicknamed the type 'Whistling Death' as they came to fear the noise made by air rushing through the diving Corsair's cooler vents heralding a deadly attack. By the end of World War II the Corsair's total tally had increased to 2,140 enemy aircraft – an 11:1 'kill'

LEFT: As well as being a superlative fighter, the Corsair was a most effective ground-attack aircraft and could carry a number of rockets beneath the wings. In the early 1950s Vought were still producing attack versions of the outstanding fighter.

ratio – destroyed in air combat with over 64,000 air combat and ground attack missions recorded.

The Corsair's first use as a carrier fighter was with Britain's Fleet Air Arm who had each of the aircraft's distinctive gull-wings clipped by around 20cm/8in to allow its stowage in the below-deck hangars on Royal Navy carriers. This debut, in April 1944, was an attack on the German battleship *Tirpitz*. The Corsair became the principal aircraft of the FAA in the Pacific and almost 2,000 were supplied to the Royal Navy and the Royal New Zealand Air Force. As FAA Corsair pilot Keith Quilter said, "In dogfights the Corsair could out-turn most contemporary aircraft and in a dive she could outrun anything."

The Corsair's outstanding performance led to extensive post-war use, notably in Korea where they flew 80 per cent of all US Navy and Marine close-support missions in the conflict's first year, 1950. Night-fighter versions were particularly successful during the conflict, and during daytime

engagements, the Corsair even engaged and destroyed Soviet-supplied MiG-15s, demonstrating along with the Hawker Sea Fury that the early jets hadn't quite left the older types behind and they were still a force to be reckoned with.

When production ceased in 1952, over 12,500 had been built giving the Corsair one of the longest US fighter production runs in history. The late F2G version was powered by the 3,000hp Pratt & Whitney R-4350 Wasp Major which was 50 per cent more powerful than the Corsair's original powerplant.

The Corsair continued to serve in the front line for a number of years and French naval pilots operated Corsairs from land bases during the anti-guerilla war against the Viet Minh in Indochina from 1952–54.

Many versions of the Corsair were built from the F4U-1 to the F4U-7. The aircraft designation differed when aircraft were produced by other manufacturers – for example, Brewster (F3A) and Goodyear (FG, F2G).

ABOVE: **Wings folded and being prepared for take-off, these Royal Navy Corsairs crowd the carrier deck. Note how much space is saved by the vertical wing-folding. The Royal Navy were the first to operate the Corsair from aircraft carriers, but the manufacturers of the aircraft had to clip the wings slightly so that they could operate from smaller British carriers.**

F4U-1 Corsair

First flight: May 29, 1940
Power: Pratt & Whitney 2,000hp R-2800-8 18-cylinder Double Wasp two-row air-cooled radial engine
Armament: Six 0.5in machine-guns with total of 2,350 rounds; C model had four M2 cannon
Size: Wingspan – 12.5m/41ft
Length – 10.15m/33ft 4in
Height – 4.9m/16ft 1in
Wing area – 29.17m^2/314sq ft
Weights: Empty – 4,074kg/8,982lb
Loaded – 6,350kg/14,000lb
Performance: Maximum speed – 671kph/417mph
Ceiling – 1,1247m/36,900ft
Range – 1,633km/1,015 miles
Climb – 881m/2,890ft per minute

LEFT: **A wheeled version of the Vought-Sikorsky OS2U-1 Kingfisher assigned to VO-3 on board the USS *Mississippi* in early 1941.** BELOW: **The Fleet Air Arm also evaluated the wheeled version under Lend-Lease arrangements, and ordered a total of 100 Kingfishers.**

BELOW: **The majority were configured as floatplanes and operated from convoys in the Atlantic and Indian Oceans. Many were also used for training in the West Indies.**

Vought-Sikorsky OS2U-3 Kingfisher

The Vought-Sikorsky OS2U Kingfisher, designed as a more versatile replacement for the O3U Corsair, was the US Navy's first catapult-launched monoplane observation floatplane. Although the aircraft was also built in tail-wheel undercarriage versions, it was mainly produced as a floatplane with one big central float and small stabilizing floats under each wing.

Despite having a comparatively low-power engine, this compact two-man aircraft served as an observation and artillery-spotting platform, anti-submarine aircraft and dive-bomber and also carried out vital rescue missions.

The first landplane and floatplane prototypes flew in March and May 1938 respectively and, following evaluation, the type was put into production in April 1940. The USS *Colorado* was the first US Navy ship to be equipped with OS2Us.

It was an OS2U that rescued US national hero Captain Eddie Rickenbacker when the B-17 in which he was flying had to ditch in the Pacific in 1942. Rickenbacker and two crewmembers were picked up but the over-laden aircraft was unable to take off. Instead the resourceful OS2U pilot taxied the aircraft on the ocean surface

over 64km/40 miles to land. In 1944 an OS2U, flying from a battleship, landed in choppy seas to pick up ten downed pilots over a period of six hours, taxiing as far as 32km/20 miles to deliver them to an Allied submarine.

The Fleet Air Arm acquired a total of 100 OS2U-3s under Lend-Lease in mid-1942, designating them Kingfisher Is. These FAA machines were used as catapult-launched observation aircraft and as trainers.

Over 1,500 were built and in addition to US Navy and Royal Navy service, the type was also operated by the US Coast Guard and air arms of Chile, Argentina, Australia, Dominican Republic and Uruguay. Four OS2Us are known to survive today, all in the USA.

Vought-Sikorsky OS2U-3 Kingfisher

First flight: May 19, 1938 (floatplane prototype)
Power: One Pratt & Whitney 459hp Wasp Junior R-985-SB-3 engine
Armament: Two 0.3in machine-guns, one forward-firing, one on mount in rear cockpit plus up to 295kg/650lb of bombs under wings
Size: Wingspan – 10.95m/35ft 11in
　　　Length – 10.31m/33ft 10in
　　　Height – 4.61m/15ft 2in
　　　Wing area – 24.34m²/262sq ft
Weights: Empty – 1,870kg/4,123lb
　　　Maximum take-off – 2,722kg/6,000lb
Performance: Maximum speed – 264kph/164mph
　　　Ceiling – 3,960m/13,000ft
　　　Range – 1,296km/805 miles
　　　Climb – 3,048m/10,000ft in 29 minutes, 6 seconds

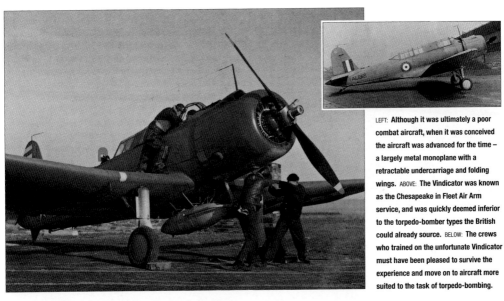

LEFT: **Although it was ultimately a poor combat aircraft, when it was conceived the aircraft was advanced for the time – a largely metal monoplane with a retractable undercarriage and folding wings.** ABOVE: **The Vindicator was known as the Chesapeake in Fleet Air Arm service, and was quickly deemed inferior to the torpedo-bomber types the British could already source.** BELOW: **The crews who trained on the unfortunate Vindicator must have been pleased to survive the experience and move on to aircraft more suited to the task of torpedo-bombing.**

Vought–Sikorsky SB2U Vindicator

The SB2U Vindicator was designed as a carrier-based reconnaissance aircraft/dive-bomber, and combined biplane technology with a monoplane layout configuration. Lacking power and therefore vulnerable, it was not a great success.

In the mid-1930s the US Navy were still hedging their bets on the question of monoplane versus biplane combat aircraft. In late 1934, Vought received a US Navy order for two prototype aircraft, one a monoplane and one a biplane but both built to meet the same requirement for a USN carrier-based scout bomber.

In testing, the XSB2U-1 monoplane proved superior and production began in October 1936. The SB2U-1 had folding outer wings, retractable landing gear, an all-metal structure covered in fabric and metal and an arrester hook for carrier operations. In theory, when it entered service in 1937 the SB2U-1 was a major step forward for the US Navy. However, the addition of essential combat equipment and armour added greatly to the weight thus affecting performance. Although obsolete by 1940, the type did see action in the Pacific (including the

Battle of Midway) with disastrous results – of the SB2Us in USN service some 30 per cent were lost in combat while a further 50 per cent suffered damage or destruction during operational training and carrier deck landing on Lake Michigan. Ironically the only surviving example, currently displayed at the US National Museum of Naval Aviation, was recovered from the bed of Lake Michigan and restored for display. By the end of 1942, US Navy SB2Us had largely been replaced by the Douglas SBD Dauntless.

Between May 1938 and July 1941, 169 SB2Us were produced. Britain's Fleet Air Arm received 50 examples, delivered between June and August 1941, but only one front-line unit, 811 Squadron, was equipped with the type. Named Chesapeake in British service, it proved to be inadequate for its intended torpedo-bomber role, in no small way due to the long take-off run required to get the underpowered aircraft to lift off a carrier deck.

In 1940, French export versions saw some action against invading German forces.

Vought-Sikorsky SB2U-1 Vindicator

First flight: January 4, 1936 (XSB2U-1 prototype)
Power: One Pratt & Whitney 825hp R-1535-96 piston engine
Armament: One fixed forward-firing 0.3in machine-gun and one 0.3in machine-gun in rear cockpit plus up to 454kg/1,000lb of bombs
Size: Wingspan – 12.8m/42ft
  Length – 10.36m/34ft
  Height – 3.12m/10ft 3in
  Wing area – 28.33m²/305sq ft
Weights: Empty – 2,121kg/4,676lb
  Maximum take-off – 3,301kg/7,278lb
Performance: Maximum speed – 402kph/250mph
  Ceiling – 8,352m/27,400ft
  Range – 1,615km/1,004 miles
  Climb – 457m/1,500ft per minute

LEFT: **Inspired by Germany's Heinkel He 118, the Yokosuka D4Y Suisei had a total production run of over 2,000. The type sealed a dubious place in aviation history as being the first aircraft used for a planned kamikaze attack.**

Yokosuka D4Y Suisei

Yokosuka was the location for the Imperial Japanese Navy's First Naval Air Technical Arsenal which in 1938 began to design a carrier-based single-engine dive-bomber. Japan had a good relationship with Germany as both powers were rapidly expanding their military potential in distant parts of the world but with common potential enemies. Co-operation took many forms including some technology sharing.

Japan was allowed to buy one of the Germany's Heinkel He 118 prototypes, the V4, and the rights to develop the He 118 concept. During a test flight the German machine, powered by a Daimler-Benz DB 601Aa, achieved a level speed of 418kph/260mph and so impressed the Japanese Navy they immediately planned for a Japanese carrier-borne version of the He 118. The requirements for this type were laid out in the 1938 Japanese Navy Experimental Carrier Bomber requirement that included a level speed of 518kph/322mph, a range of

2,222km/1,381 miles without a bomb, and a range of 1,482km/921 miles with a bomb load of 250kg/551lb.

Headed by Masao Yamana, the Yokosuka design team created a single-engine, two-seat, mid-wing monoplane dive-bomber with a fully retractable 'taildragger' landing gear. With a wingspan similar to that of the Mitsubishi A6M, the Yokosuka machine did not need heavy, expensive wing-folding gear, thereby reducing maintenance needs too. Designated D4Y1 Suisei (Comet), the aircraft was unusual as it was one of few Japanese combat types to be powered by a liquid-cooled Aichi AE1 Atsuta piston engine, which was the Japanese licence-built derivative of the German Daimler Benz 601.

Although the basic configuration showed a resemblance to the Heinkel machine, the D4Y design was smaller, lighter, stronger and was altogether a more advanced design that benefited from the increasing understanding of aerodynamics.

ABOVE: **The very distinctive nose arrangement of the early D4Ys, reminiscent of a Junkers Ju 87 Stuka, was due to the use of licence-built versions of the German liquid-cooled piston engine. Note the telescope sight in front of the cockpit, for dive-bombing targeting.**

LEFT: **Ground crew await the instruction to remove chocks as this D4Y1 prepares for flight. Note the use of two underwing auxiliary fuel tanks to boost the aircraft's range.** ABOVE: **The D4Y was comparatively slow and was vulnerable to enemy fighters and anti-aircraft artillery.**

The aircraft's main weapon was a 500kg/1,102lb bomb carried internally. The first D4Y1 prototype made its maiden flight in December 1940, and was found to possess an excellent combination of high performance and good handling. Despite this promising start during dive-bombing trials, the wings demonstrated 'flutter', a high-frequency oscillation of the structure, which was sufficient to crack the wing spar. With the aircraft unfit for the task it was designed for, the pre-production version was instead switched to reconnaissance duties, due to its good speed, range and ceiling. The aircraft served in this role from autumn 1942 until the war's end as the D4Y1-C. The dedicated dive-bomber version – the D4Y1 fitted with catapult equipment to operate from smaller Japanese carriers – finally entered service in 1943. The latter version took part in the June 1944 air-sea engagements off the Marianas, becoming the victim in what US pilots named 'The Great Marianas Turkey Shoot'.

Although the Yokosuka dive-bomber generally displayed good performance, excellent range and manoeuvrability, all versions had insufficient armour protection for the crew, and the type's light construction was unable to take much battle damage. These were faults common to many Japanese combat aircraft. The type did not fare well against high-performance Allied fighters, and many fell to their guns – partly due to the lack of self-sealing fuel tanks.

It was the D4Y of Rear Admiral Arima, commanding officer of 26th Koku Sentai, that carried out what is believed to be the first planned suicide kamikaze mission when it flew into the carrier USS *Franklin* on October 15, 1944.

A total of 2,038 were built. The D4Y2 was given a more powerful engine, while the D4Y4 was a bomber version that carried one 800kg/1,764lb bomb and was used in kamikaze missions. The Allied codename allocated to all versions was 'Judy'.

ABOVE: **The D4Y3 was an improved D4Y2 powered by a 1,560hp Mitsubishi radial engine. This required a remodelling of the nose and made the aircraft look very different to the earlier in-line engined versions.**

Yokosuka D4Y2

First flight: November, 1940
Power: One Aichi 1,400hp Atsuta 32 piston engine
Armament: Two 7.7mm forward-firing machine-guns and one 7.92mm rear-firing machine-gun plus up to 800kg/1,763lb of bombs
Size: Wingspan –11.5m/37ft 8.75in
Length –10.22m/33ft 6.25in
Height – 3.74m/12ft 3.25in
Wing area – 23.6m²/254sq ft
Weights: Empty – 2,440kg/5,379lb
Maximum take-off – 4,250kg/9,370lb
Performance: Maximum speed – 550kph/342mph
Service ceiling – 10,700m/35,105ft
Range – 1,465km/910 miles
Climb – 820m/2,700ft per minute

Glossary

AAF Army Air Forces.

aerodynamics Study of how gases, including air, flow and how forces act upon objects moving through air.

AEW Airborne Early Warning.

ailerons Control surfaces at trailing edge of each wing used to make the aircraft roll.

angle of attack Angle of a wing to the oncoming airflow.

ASV Air-to-Surface-Vessel – pertaining to this type of radar developed during World War II.

ASW Anti-Submarine Warfare.

biplane An aircraft with two sets of wings.

blister A streamlined, often clear, large fairing on aircraft body housing guns or electronics.

CAP Combat Air Patrol.

ceiling The maximum height at which an aircraft can operate.

dihedral The upward angle of the wing formed where the wings connect to the fuselage.

dorsal Pertaining to the upper side of an aircraft.

drag The force that resists the motion of the aircraft through the air.

ECM Electronic Counter Measures.

elevators Control surfaces on the horizontal part of the tail that are used to alter the aircraft's pitch.

FAA Fleet Air Arm.

fin The vertical portion of the tail.

flaps Moveable parts of the trailing edge of a wing used to increase lift at slower air speeds.

hp Horsepower.

IFF Identification Friend or Foe.

jet engine An engine that works by creating a high-velocity jet of air to propel the engine forward.

leading edge The front edge of a wing or tailplane.

monoplane An aircraft with one set of wings.

pitch Rotational motion in which an aircraft turns around its lateral axis.

port Left side.

RAAF Royal Australian Air Force.

radome Protective covering for radar made from material through which radar beams can pass.

RAF Royal Air Force.

RATO Rocket-Assisted Take-Off.

RCAF Royal Canadian Air Force.

RFC Royal Flying Corps.

RN Royal Navy.

RNAS Royal Naval Air Service.

roll Rotational motion in which the aircraft turns around its longitudinal axis.

rudder The parts of the tail surfaces that control an aircraft's yaw (its left and right turning).

starboard Right side.

tailplane Horizontal part of the tail, known as horizontal stabilizer in North America.

thrust Force produced by engine which pushes an aircraft forward.

triplane An aircraft with three sets of wings.

UHF Ultra High Frequency.

USAAC United States Army Air Corps.

USAAF United States Army Air Forces.

USAF United States Air Force.

USCG United States Coast Guard.

USMC United States Marine Corps.

USN United States Navy.

ventral Pertaining to the underside of an aircraft.

VHF Very High Frequency.

Key to flags

For the specification boxes, the national flag that was current at the time of the aircraft's use is shown.

 Germany

 Italy

 Japan

 UK

 USA

Acknowledgements

The publisher would like to thank the following individuals and picture libraries for the use of their pictures in the book. Every effort has been made to acknowledge the pictures properly, however we apologize if there are any unintentional omissions, which will be corrected in future editions.

l=left, r=right, t=top, b=bottom, m=middle, um = upper middle, lm= lower middle

Michael J.F. Bowyer: 63b.

Francis Crosby Collection: 7t, 7br, 8–9, 13ml, 14b, 15t, 15b, 22t, 22b, 23um, 23bl, 23br, 37bl, 37br, 39t, 40m, 41t, 41m, 42b, 44tr, 54t, 55m, 59tl, 59tr, 59b, 60t, 60b, 61t, 61m, 61b, 62m, 62b, 63t, 63m, 65b, 66t, 66b, 67b, 72bl, 72br, 74bl, 74br, 75m, 76m, 79tl, 80tr, 80b, 81t, 81m, 81b, 83tl, 95m, 96t, 96b, 97tl, 97tr, 97b, 102b, 103tl, 103tr, 108t, 108m, 109b, 111b, 113t, 114tr, 115t, 115m, 115b, 116tl, 116tr, 116b, 117m, 118tr, 118b, 119b, 120tr, 120b, 121tl, 121tr, 121b.

Chris Farmer: 23t, 40b, 46t, 47t, 55t, 62t, 67tl, 72t, 75b.

Brian Marsh: 117t.

TRH Pictures: 1, 2, 3, 5, 6t, 6b, 7bl, 10t, 10b, 11t, 11m, 12t, 12b, 13tl, 13tr, 13b, 14t, 15m, 16t, 16b, 17tl, 17tr, 17m, 17b, 18t, 18b, 19tl, 19tr, 19m, 19b, 20tl, 20tr, 21tl, 21tr, 21bl, 21br, 24t, 24b, 25t, 25ml, 25mr, 25b, 28t, 28bl, 28br, 29t, 29m, 29b, 30t, 30b, 31tl, 31tr, 31m, 31b, 32t, 32b, 33tl, 33tr, 33b, 34t, 34b, 35tl, 35tr, 35b, 36t, 36b, 37t, 37m, 38t, 38b, 39m, 39b, 40t, 42t, 42m, 43t, 43b, 44tl, 44b, 45t, 45b, 46bl, 46br, 47m, 48t, 48b, 49tl, 49tr, 49b, 50t, 50bl, 50br, 51t, 51m, 51b, 52t, 52m, 52b, 53tl, 53tr, 53b, 54b, 55b, 56tl, 56tr, 56b, 57t, 57m, 57b, 58tl, 58tr, 58b, 64t, 64b, 65t, 65m, 66m, 68tl, 68tr, 68b, 69tl, 69tr, 69b, 70tl, 70tr, 70b, 71tl, 71tr, 71b, 73tl, 73tr, 74t, 75t, 76t, 76b, 77tl, 77tr, 77b, 78b, 79tr, 79m, 82tl, 82tr, 82b, 103tr, 83b, 84tl, 84tr, 84b, 85t, 85m, 85b, 86tl, 86tr, 86b, 87t, 87m, 87b, 88t, 88m, 88b, 89t, 89m, 89b, 90t, 90b, 91tl, 91tr, 91b, 92t, 92b, 93t, 93m, 93b, 94t, 94b, 95t, 95b, 98t, 98b, 99tl, 99tr, 99m, 99b, 100t, 100b, 101t, 101m, 101b, 102tl, 102tr, 103b, 104t, 104b, 105tl, 105tr, 105b, 106tl, 106tr, 106b, 107t, 107bl, 107br, 108b, 109t, 110t, 110m, 110b, 111t, 111m, 112t, 112b, 113b, 114tl, 114b, 117b, 119t, 120tl, 122t, 122b, 123tl, 123tr, 123b, 124, 125, 126, 127 128, endpapers.

Nick Waller: 11b, 44–5, 41b, 47b, 67tr, 73b, 77m, 78t, 79b, 80tl, 118tl, 118m.

Index